GREAT CANADIAN
BATTLES

HEROISM AND COURAGE THROUGH THE YEARS

EDWARD HUMPHREYS

ARCTURUS

This edition published in 2014 by Arcturus Publishing Limited
26/27 Bickels Yard, 151–153 Bermondsey Street,
London SE1 3HA

AD003887EN

Printed in the UK

CONTENTS

INTRODUCTION

On 29 OCTOBER 1813, *'dans le bois en haut de la rivière Châteauguay'*, Lieutenant Colonel Charles-Michel d'Irumberry de Salaberry wrote to his father about *'un événement fort extraordinaire'*. Three days earlier, Salaberry had led a force consisting of fewer than 500 militia to victory over more than 4,000 American regulars. The Battle of the Châteauguay, as the clash became known, was one of the most significant of the War of 1812. Salaberry's great triumph shocked the republic to the south and put an end to their ambitions concerning Montreal. The capture of the city, so crucial to the American effort, would forever remain beyond their grasp.

The Battle of the Châteauguay was part of a conflict which began when the United States declared war on the 'United Kingdom of Great Britain and Ireland and the Dependencies Thereof'. British North America provided the settings of many of the conflict's greatest battles.

Those living on the soil of what would one day become the Dominion of Canada were expected to fight for their mother country, just as they had in the Seven Years' War, and just as they would in the Second Boer War and the First World War. The identity of the mother country was dependent entirely on the time. As his father had done during the American War of Independence, Salaberry fought for the British against the armies of the United States of America. Yet, Charles-Michel d'Irumberry de Salaberry's grandfather served as lieutenant commander of the French frigate *Fidèle* fighting Great Britain's Royal Navy at the Battle of Louisbourg.

The hero of the Battle of the Châteauguay considered himself Canadian, as did the men who were under his command. In fact, the battle was the largest of the war to have been fought exclusively by those who had been born in what would 54 years later become the Dominion of Canada. Many of those who defended British North America in the War of 1812 were British regulars. Indeed, some of the great battles in pre-Confederation Canadian history, events of significance and ramification, were fought, in the main, by foreign soldiers. Beginning with the *fin de siècle* Second Boer War the situation reversed. In that war and all that followed, it was the Canadians who were the foreign soldiers fighting overseas.

Any study of military conflict is also a lesson in history. The battles included in this book reflect the ever-changing geopolitical landscape. It is in this environment that the Salaberry family switched its allegiance from France to their old enemy the British. The United States of America, for more than a century a threat to Canadians, would become an ally in the First World War, the Second World War, the Korean War, the Gulf War and the war in Afghanistan.

The Canadians fighting at the Battle of the Châteauguay numbered fewer than 500, and yet their actions altered the course of the histories of both Canada and the United States, testimony that a battle need not feature large numbers of soldiers to prove itself influential and significant. Indeed, several of these great Canadian battles were little more than skirmishes, lasting no more than minutes, causing no real damage or destruction. At this distance, some, such as the Battle of Montgomery's Tavern, might appear comical were it not for the loss of life, however small that number.

Led by a newspaperman and fought in a provincial capital, The Battle of Yonge Street is fairly well documented. The same cannot be said of every engagement, no matter how significant. The only first-hand account of the Battle of Lake Champlain – fewer than 300 words – was penned by Samuel de Champlain, the very man to first use firearms in warfare against the First Nations. Of earlier Canadian battles we must rely, for the most part, on archaeologists and the narratives of native storytellers.

Great bravery, victory and loss provide strong threads from which legends are woven. Thus, while the Battle of Yonge Street has been relegated to history books, the battles of the Plains of Abraham, Queenston Heights and Vimy Ridge have taken their places in the Canadian psyche and culture. Other great stories of heroism, such as Salaberry's victory at the Châteauguay river, have never been properly recognized. This is, perhaps, too modest a country.

Edward Humphreys

CHAPTER I

— ◆ —

The Wars *of* New France

THE WARS *of* NEW FRANCE

An introduction

THE HISTORY OF New France is not a peaceful one; its survival was accompanied by conflict and death. Seeking trade and security for their tenuous settlements, the earliest French settlers soon found themselves caught in the midst of ongoing tribal warfare. Samuel de Champlain's reliance on the Algonquian-speaking tribes brought an alliance which would lead to war with the rival Iroquois Confederacy.

During the first half of the 17th century the French and Iroquois War came very close to destroying New France. It lasted until the Great Peace of Montreal, a peace treaty signed after 92 years of war by Governor Louis-Hector de Callière and more than 1,200 representatives of 39 First Nations.

By necessity, New France was a militarized society. Its few significant settlements – Quebec, Montreal, Trois-Rivières, Port-Royale and Louisbourg – were surrounded by fortifications. For much of its history, it required that its Canadian males, aged 16 to 60, join militia companies and be trained in the art of war.

As France expanded its territory in North America, so too did Great Britain. By the middle of the 17th century, competing claims led to small skirmishes and, on occasion, bloodshed. However, the first North American war between the French and the British – King William's War – was not the result of territorial aspirations, but conflict in Europe. In fact, 'King William's War' was nothing but a name used by the colonialists of New England in reference to the North American theatre of the War of the Grand Alliance. Fought from 1689 until 1697, King William's War resulted in the deaths of several hundred people, a great many victims of massacre.

Early in the fighting, the British captured Port-Royale. Though it was held without challenge for the balance of the war, the capital of Acadia was returned to the French through the Treaty of Ryswick. Thirteen years later, during Queen Anne's War (the North American branch of the War of the Spanish Succession), the town was again captured. At the end of the conflict, with the signing of the 1713 Treaty of Utrecht, France lost peninsular Nova Scotia, Newfoundland and its territory around Hudson Bay. After 27 years of peace, the longest in its history, in 1740 New France entered into King George's War, an eight-year conflict that was part of the War of the Austrian Succession.

There followed six years of peace before New France began fighting what would be its ultimate war. Unlike the others, the Seven Years' War began prior to the larger European conflict with which it became attached. More than 8,000 – nearly one in seven of New France's 60,000 citizens – served; casualties amounted to more than 2,000.

By the time of the Treaty of Paris on 10 February 1763, in which New France was brought to an end with the ceding of nearly all of France's North American territory to Great Britain, the colony had been at war for 37 of its last 74 years.

THE BATTLE *of* LAKE CHAMPLAIN

30 JULY 1609

———•———

AN EXPLORER, navigator and gifted carto-grapher, Samuel de Champlain is remembered above all as the 'Father of New France'. By founding Quebec City on 3 July 1608, he secured French dominance of the Saint Lawrence river – '*la rivière du Canada*' – for more than 150 years.

Champlain had first explored the Saint Lawrence in the spring and summer of 1603, a journey that brought him into contact with the Montagnais, Huron and Algonquin peoples. In doing so, he entered a long-standing war between the Algonquian-speaking tribes of the Great Lakes region and the Iroquois Confederacy to the south of the river. Intent on maintaining and growing a fur trade, Champlain chose to ally himself with the former. It would, however, be many years before a Frenchman – Champlain himself – would participate in the violence of the ongoing struggle.

Despite having struck this vague alliance, the French were quite content to let the war between the Great Lakes Native Americans and the Iroquois Confederacy play out. However, by 1609, Champlain was increasingly troubled by reports that the Iroquois were disrupting his Native American partners in the fur trade.

On 7 June, he left Quebec and travelled more than 2,000 km downriver to Tadoussac, where he met with Gravé Du Pont, a '*noble homme*' and administrator for New France. The two men discussed the possibilities of arbitrating a peace treaty; or possibly reverting their own position to one of neutrality, which would allow for trade with both groups. Champlain and Du Pont concluded that a negotiated peace between the Algonquian-speaking Native Americans and the Iroquois Confederacy was impossible; French neutrality, they determined, would be viewed by the Iroquois as a sign of weakness, and might very well transform allies into enemies.

The following month, accompanied by two unnamed

Frenchmen and a good number of Montagnais, Huron and Algonquin warriors, Champlain set out up the River of the Iroquois, now known as the Richelieu river. This new expedition appealed to two sides of Champlain's character. He had been told of a great lake – *Caniaderiguaronte*, 'the lake that is the gateway to the country' – to the south; and, beyond that, another long river. However, all this lay within or beyond territory controlled by the Iroquois Confederacy, and would likely lead to conflict. Thus, Champlain's great love of exploration met with his business interests.

After a few days' travel, without incident, Champlain finally saw the great lake about which he had heard from his Algonquian-speaking allies. He described the body of water in his 1613 book *Voyages* as containing 'fine islands', 'bordered by many fine trees', and 'containing a great abundance of fish, of many varieties'. Clearly overcome by the lake, which he estimated as being 'eighty or a hundred leagues long' – two to three times its actual length – Champlain threw off the Native American name and modestly rechristened the body of water after himself.

Champlain would never see the long river that lay beyond his lake. Late on the evening of 29 July, out on the waters, he and his party encountered a group of Iroquois warriors. As they drew near, the Iroquois moved to the shore and began constructing barricades with their canoes and trees cut down with crude stone axes. Champlain's war party dispatched two canoes to the enemy and inquired as to whether they were willing to fight. According to the French explorer, the response was 'that they wanted nothing else'. It was agreed that, it being too dark to fight, the battle would take place at sunrise the following day.

With the Iroquois on the shore, Champlain's men fastened their canoes together and waited. The two war parties spent the evening within earshot of one another, singing, bragging and trading insults. Among the boasts Champlain's men hurled at the Iroquois on shore was that they would soon witness 'such execution of arms as never before'.

The following day, after donning light armour, Champlain led his Native American war party towards the shore. While still on the water, he witnessed nearly 200 Iroquois warriors leaving their barricade, advancing at a slow pace. At the front were the three chiefs, so distinguished by their headdresses. Champlain was advised by members of his war party that these Iroquois leaders should be killed if at all possible.

The only first-hand account of the battle is that provided by Champlain himself, in his *Voyages*:

> As soon as we had landed, they began to run for some two hundred paces towards their enemies, who stood firmly, not having as yet noticed my companions, who went into the woods with some savages. Our men began to call me with loud cries; and in order to give me a passage-way, they opened in two parts, and put me at their head, where I marched some twenty paces in advance of the rest, until I was within about thirty paces of the enemy, who at once noticed me, and, halting, gazed at me, as I did also at them. When I saw them making a move to fire at us, I rested my musket against my cheek, and aimed directly at one of the three chiefs. With the same shot, two fell to the

ground; and one of their men was so wounded that he died some time after. I had loaded my musket with four balls. When our side saw this shot so favourable for them, they began to raise such loud cries that one could not have heard it thunder. Meanwhile, the arrows flew on both sides. The Iroquois were greatly astonished that two men had been so quickly killed, although they were equipped with armour woven from cotton thread, and with wood which was a proof against their arrows. This caused great alarm among them. As I was loading again, one of my companions fired a shot from the woods, which astonished them anew to such a degree that, seeing their chiefs dead, they lost courage, and took to flight, abandoning their camp and fort, and fleeing into the woods, whither I pursued them, killing still more of them. Our savages also killed several of them, and took ten or twelve prisoners. The remainder escaped with the wounded. Fifteen or sixteen were wounded on our side with arrow-shots; but they were soon healed.

The account of Champlain's battle on the lake he named after himself was for a time featured prominently in adventure stories written for Canadian boys. That time has now passed; even his own account seems now less than honourable.

While it is not possible to judge the accuracy of Champlain's description, there are certain flaws in his account of the voyage up the River of the Iroquois and exploration of Lake Champlain. Dates are incorrect, descriptions are exaggerated and, in the case of a fish said to be 5 feet long and featuring a double row of teeth, fanciful.

About the battle itself, the only thing that can be said with certainty is that it did not take place at Crown Point; his description of the area quite clearly indicates Ticonderoga as being the actual site of battle.

The shots fired by Champlain at Ticonderoga would have serious consequences for New France. Anything but a serious defeat for the Iroquois Confederacy, it only served to anger and solidify an alliance with the British, France's rival on the continent. New France suffered for nearly a century from raids, sieges and battles brought by the Iroquois. In

1701, peace between the colony and the Confederacy was finally struck with the signing of the Great Peace of Montreal. Yet, the treaty did not cleanse the bitterness that existed within the Iroquois people. The ill-feeling towards New France continued for more than half a century. During the Seven Years' War, the Iroquois fought on the side of the British, and in doing so finally brought an end to France's great North American colony.

THE BATTLE *of* QUEBEC

18–19 OCTOBER 1690

———•———

THE ONLY REMAINING fortified North American city in Canada and the United States during the first half of its 400 years, Quebec endured numerous threats. It had been attacked by the British, the French and the Americans. As capital of New France, the town was the site of what is without argument the most famous battle to be fought on Canadian soil: the Battle of the Plains of Abraham. That particular struggle, between forces under General James Wolfe and General Louis-Joseph de Montcalm-Gozon is sometimes referred to as the Second Battle of Quebec. It followed, by nearly seven decades, the very first assault on the town, an event which took place during the War of the Grand Alliance.

The conflict began in May of 1689 after England's William III joined the League of Augsburg to form the Grand Alliance against France. Under the name King

William's War, fighting in the North American theatre began three months later when 1,500 Iroquois attacked the French settlement at La Chine – present day Lachine – on the Island of Montreal.

New France retaliated with assaults on the Iroquois village of Onondaga and on English frontier settlements, most notably the Schenectady Massacre of 1690 in which 12 children, 10 women and 38 men were killed.

This and other horrors were overshadowed on 19 May 1690 by the first significant large-scale battle of the North American campaign. Seven warships, carrying 736 men from England's Massachusetts Bay colony, attacked Port-Royal – present-day Annapolis Royal – the capital of the French colony of Acadia. With its 70-man garrison taken by surprise, its fortifications in a state of disrepair and its cannons unmounted, Port-Royal was taken without a fight. Led by their commander Major General Sir William Phips, the New Englanders plundered the settlement before returning with hostages to their base in Boston, leaving a puppet government behind.

After the capture of Acadia's capital, emboldened New Englanders set their sights on New France. An overland expedition involving New Yorkers intent on seizing Montreal was weak and amounted to nothing. As it failed, a much grander expedition, featuring 2,300 militia was being organized at the Massachusetts Bay colony for an assault on Quebec. Command would again fall upon Phips.

Financed through paper bonds set against the expected plunder to be gained at the capital of New France, the operation was not atypical of the major general. A man of no education, his fortunes began to change when he married a wealthy widow. He then embarked on a career as a treasure hunter, recovering sunken valuables in the waters of the Caribbean. One venture, off the coast of Haiti in 1687, earned his investors nearly £200.

Phips' planned assault on Quebec involved a total of 32 ships, of which four were significant in size. His departure for New France was delayed by a lengthy wait for supplies. These were meant to have been sent from England, but never arrived. It was not until 19 August that Phips finally set sail from Hull, some 15 km to the south-east of Boston. As the flotilla made its way up the Atlantic Coast to the Gulf of Saint Lawrence and up the river itself, it was delayed further by inclement weather, contrary winds and unfamiliarity with the waters on which they sailed.

On 16 October, after a voyage of 58 days, the first of Phips' ships dropped anchor in the Quebec basin.

The major general lost no time in dispatching an envoy, Major Thomas Savage, to meet with the Governor General of New France, Louis de Buade, Compte de Frontenac et de Paluau. Savage was led blindfold through the streets of Quebec past jeering crowds, a tactic which served to exaggerate the number of citizens within the fortified town. At the Château Saint-Louis, before Frontenac and his officers, the envoy delivered a summons of surrender. When finished, Savage informed the inhabitants that they had one hour in which to act in accordance with the demands of the New Englanders. As the envoy awaited a responses, Frontenac spoke: '*Non, je n'ai point de réponse à faire à votre général que par la bouche de mes canons et de mes fusils.*'

The governor general wanted to have Savage hanged within view of the Massachusetts Bay fleet, and was prevented from doing so only through the intercession of François de Laval, the Bishop of Quebec.

Savage returned to Phips and delivered Frontenac's response.

The major general had little regard for the French and the citizens of their colonies. Phips regarded the bloodless victory at Port-Royal as confirmation of his belief that they were militarily unable.

In this, the unschooled treasure hunter was very much mistaken. Since the advent of King William's War, aided by the Sault and Algonquin, the French had been waging a successful campaign against the Iroquois and the New Englanders. Frontenac, their governor general, was a highly educated, experienced man who had fought in the Low Countries and Italy. Under his leadership, a wooden palisade had been built to enclose the town. This fortification was supported by 11 stone redoubts and a heavily constructed windmill in which a three-gun battery had been installed.

Eight cannons had been mounted beside the Château, with six more at the docks; all faced the Saint Lawrence.

In preparation for the battle with Phips, Frontenac summoned his militia – a force of almost 3,000 – adding to three battalions of colonial regulars. Temporary obstacles were placed on the road leading to the upper town.

Watching Phips and his amateur soldiers from his fortified town atop the cliffs, Frontenac could not have felt anything but extreme confidence.

The New Englanders' plan, struck by a council of war, was to have some 1,200 men land at Beauport, on the eastern shore of the Saint Charles river. From there, with the use of the fleet's boats, they would cross the river, carrying the field guns. Once the large landing force had gained the heights to the west of Quebec, the fleet would attack and land a second force at the front of the town.

However, Frontenac had anticipated an assault from Beauport, and had had the field fortifications built on the south-west side.

Charged with the main assault, Phips' second-in-command, Major John Walley, was prevented from crossing the Saint Charles by detachments of Canadian militiamen and Native American warriors. Commanded by Jacques Le Moyne de Sainte-Hélène, they positioned themselves in the wooded areas along the eastern shore, from which they fired on the New Englanders. Meanwhile, the accompanying ships mistakenly landed their cannons on the wrong side of the river.

All was taking place as the four large ships of the flotilla, contrary to plans, began bombarding the town.

Inadequately supplied to begin with, by the next day the best part of the New Englanders' ammunition had been spent. Damage wrought by their cannons paled beside that they had suffered from Quebec's shore batteries. Many of the ships, including the flagship *Six Friends*, were badly damaged. One of the smaller ships had been captured with the aid of a single canoe by a small group of Canadians.

During all this time, the land force on the eastern shore of the Saint Charles had remained inactive. On 20 October, having suffered two days of cold and shortages of food and rum, Walley decided to launch a European-style assault on Frontenac's earthworks.

The attack was met with heavy fire, killing more than 30 of the Massachusetts Bay force. The Canadians suffered only a handful of casualties, though one of these was Sainte-Hélène, who was mortally wounded. There folowed two more days of futility before Walley's force withdrew, abandoning five cannons in the process.

After negotiating an exchange of prisoners, Phips set sail for the Massachusetts Bay colony. The autumnal passage was anything but pleasant. Phips lost an estimated 1,000 men to smallpox, drowning and fire; ten of his returning fleet were destroyed. One rather improbable account has it that a ship was wrecked off Anticosti Island, where the crew endured a winter before being rescued the following summer.

In failing to provide his forces with adequate supplies of food, drink and ammunition, Phips had revealed himself as an incompetent planner. The lack of leadership demonstrated during the Battle of Quebec exposed his negligible military talents. His bloodless taking of Port-Royal came to be seen as an aberration, not an accomplishment.

Yet, the disastrous defeat at Quebec appeared to have no influence on his career. The year after the battle he was granted a charter by William III. In 1692, he was installed as the first royal governor of Massachusetts Bay. It was in this position that he advised against a proposed 1693 seaborne expedition against Quebec.

The Battle of Quebec was the first test of the town's defences. Although the fortification itself had not been approached, Frontenac determined that significant improvements would be required to defend against a serious European-style siege. In the summer of 1693, wholesale construction began on new defences.

For the British, Phips' failure rested on incompetence and scope. It was recognized that any successful assault on Quebec would require trained regulars and sizeable warships. It wasn't until 1711 that Great Britain attempted to capture Quebec. There would be no battle.

What became known as 'The Walker Expedition to Quebec' ended in disaster when a store ship and seven transports were wrecked off the northern coast of the Gulf of Saint Lawrence. Nearly 900 men drowned or died from exposure. The operation was abandoned, leaving the citizens of Quebec, more than 1,000 km to the south-west, unaware that there had been any threat to their town.

CHAPTER II

— ◆ —

The Seven Years' War

THE WAR *for* NORTH AMERICA
1754–60
An introduction

SIR WINSTON CHURCHILL considered the Seven Years' War to be the true First World War. Like the 1914–18 conflict, it involved very nearly every European power and, through their colonies, spread beyond the continent.

The trigger of the war, Prussia's invasion of Saxony, rested on the complexities and vagaries of succession, diplomacy and alliances which had seen much of the political map of Europe redrawn in the first half of the 18th century. To those fighting in North America, however, the cause and purpose of their battles appeared quite clear. The war was yet another in the century-long struggle between the kingdoms of France and Great Britain for control of the continent. Ultimately, the Seven Years' War would determine the future of both empires in the New World.

While significant parts of a greater conflict, there is a tendency within Canada and the United States to consider the North American battles separately. This propensity might best be explained by geography and the powers involved. Where the European war had 14 major belligerents – Prussia, Great Britain, France, Portugal, Austria, Sweden, Spain, Sardinia, Russia, the Kingdom of Naples and Sicily, and the Electorates of Hanover, Brunswick, Hesse-Kassel and Saxony – in North America, the fighting was limited to just Great Britain, France and their traditional First Nations allies.

Another great difference between the European and North American theatres is that the hostility in the latter had earlier begin and end dates. The first conflict in North America's Seven Years' War occurred on 28 May 1754, when French and British militia fought at the Battle of Jumonville Glen in what is present-day Pennsylvania. The cause of the clash has always been in dispute. Commanded by Lieutenant Colonel George Washington, the future revolutionary leader, the British claimed to have been fired upon by the French. This story was challenged by French survivors, who accused Washington and his men of having ambushed their encampment. Whatever the story, it would appear that the force of 31 French Canadians was very much at a disadvantage. During a battle which lasted only 15 minutes, ten militiamen were killed and the other 21 were taken prisoner. All but one of the captured, including their commander, Ensign Joseph Coulen de Villiers de Jumonville, were later massacred by Washington's troops and their bodies left to the wolves.

The precise nature of Jumonville's mission has been one of considerable debate and speculation. To some, the French Canadian was a spy; others insist he was scouting possible locations for a new fort and still others accept the explanation given by Washington that he was a peaceful emissary sent by Louis XV. However, documentary evidence indicates that Jumonville had been dispatched to determine whether Washington had invaded territory claimed by France.

At Westminster, Washington was criticized greatly for the incident. The 18th-century British statesman Horace Walpole went so far as to identify the Battle of Jumonville Glen, and not the invasion of Saxony, as marking the beginning of the Seven Years' War. 'It was', he wrote, 'the volley fired by a young Virginian in the backwoods of America that set the world on fire.'

In the United States, the conflict is most frequently referred to as the French and Indian War – a rather curious, if inaccurate name, as it leaves out Great Britain and its colonies.

To some in Canada, the Seven Years' War is *la Guerre de la Conquête*, a recognition of the defeat of France and the loss of New France, the largest of its many colonies. At the end of the conflict, with the signing of the Treaty of Paris, France ceded nearly all its North American territory. The only exceptions were two small islands, Saint-Pierre and Miquelon, off the southern coast of Newfoundland.

THE BATTLE *of* FORT BEAUSÉJOUR
3–16 JUNE 1755

MANY BATTLES FOLLOWED that of Jumonville Glen; indeed, the Battle of Fort Necessity, fought five weeks later on 3 July 1754, was a French counter-attack. Here, Lieutenant Colonel George Washington had to contend with a force led by Sieur Louis Coulon de Villiers, the half-brother of Joseph Coulon de Villiers de Jumonville, who had been murdered while in captivity. It was an easy victory for the French.

Though not officially at war, over the course of two years, the British and French colonies of North America provided the battlegrounds of no fewer than six clashes, resulting in the deaths of more than 1,000 men. Among these battles, and the one with the greatest lasting effect was that which took place at Fort Beauséjour, near present-day Sackville, New Brunswick.

The battle began on 3 June 1755, after a fleet of Royal

Navy ships under the command of Lieutenant Colonel Robert Monckton sailed into Cumberland Basin and entered, unchallenged, the mouth of the Missaguash river. Nearly 300 British regulars and 2,000 New England militia landed, under cover of Fort Lawrence, the nearby British fort. They took up position along Aulac Ridge to the north of Fort Beauséjour and began their advance. Monckton's assault on the French was surgical; he took no chances and ensured that his force maintained discipline in the face of apparent success. When within range, the British and New Englanders began a barrage with 13-inch (33-cm) mortars.

Those serving within the French fort had the misfortune of being commanded by Louis Du Pont Duchambon de Vergor, a man who never would have achieved his position had it not been for his friendship with François Bigot, the Intendant of New France. One observer wrote of Vergor: 'He is the most dull-witted fellow I have ever met but he knows all the angles.'

Although he knew surrender to be inevitable, for 13 days Vergor stood by, inactive under the bombardment, as casualties mounted. Finally, on 16 June, after the fortification was breached by mortar fire, Fort Beauséjour was surrendered to Monckton.

The next day, the British and New Englanders took a second French stronghold, Fort Gaspareaux, 35 km northeast on Bay Verte, with no opposition.

Monckton's victory had little strategic value, and brought the British only very slightly closer to their goal of dominating North America. Its historic significance lies in the tragic effect it had on the Acadian people. Although they were the descendants of 17th-century French settlers, they had previously declared their neutrality in the ongoing struggle between France and Great Britain. However, the discovery of 300 Acadians within the surrendered fort worked to erode the fragile trust the British held. As a result, the governor of Nova Scotia, Charles Lawrence, fell back on terms that had been imposed on the Acadians at the end of Queen Anne's War: 'These Inhabitants were Permitted to Remain in Quiet Possession of their Lands, Upon Condition they Should take the Oath of Allegiance to the King within one year after the Treaty of Utrecht by which this Province was Ceded to Great Britain'. Some 42 years had passed since the treaty had been signed and now, after some Acadians were found to have 'Abetted the French Incroachments by their Treachery, the Other have Countananced them by Open Rebellion', Lawrence would insist that the oath be taken. The vast majority refused to swear allegiance to the British Crown, thus beginning *Le Grand Dérangement*, a mass deportation which ultimately involved more than 10,000 Acadians.

THE BATTLE *of* LOUISBOURG
8 JUNE – 26 JULY 1758

IN THE SIX North American battles that had taken place prior to the fighting in Europe, victories were divided evenly between Great Britain and France. Neither side made significant advances over the other. However, in the months that followed Great Britain's declaration of war on France on 15 May 1756, this balance was disturbed.

On 14 August, in the earliest battle, General Louis-Joseph de Montcalm-Gozon and a force of 3,000 seized and occupied Fort Oswego in the colony of New York. It was a decisive victory, one which resulted in the capture of 121 cannons and more than 1,700 men, and interrupted British shipping on Lake Ontario.

A year passed before the next clash between the British and the French. On 3 August 1757, Montcalm led a force of 6,000 regulars, supported by 1,600 Native American warriors, into battle at Fort William Henry on the shore of Lake George. Here again, the French general was the victor, capturing the stronghold and thwarting British plans to attack Montreal, 250 km to the north. The triumph, however, was marred by the deaths of several hundred surrendered British at the hands of Montcalm's Native American allies.

The British entered the autumn of 1757 despairing over the war in North America. After three and a half years of fighting in the colonies, more territory had been lost than gained. If there was any good news to be had it lay in the fact that British fortunes in Europe, once so dire, had greatly improved. Credit for the transformation lay with Secretary of State William Pitt, who had assumed control of the war effort the previous year. North America, he determined, required a bolder, more aggressive approach. To his foes, there could be nothing more audacious than his intended target, the Fortress of Louisbourg.

Known as 'The Gibraltar of North America', Louisbourg had been designed in accordance with the fortification theories of Sébastien Le Prestre de Vauban, the greatest military engineer of the 16th and 17th centuries. Construction began in 1719, and had continued for more than two and a half decades. Its considerable cost caused Louis XV to complain: 'Are the streets being paved with gold over there? I fully expect to awake one morning in Versailles to see the walls of the fortress rising above the horizon.' A droll remark, perhaps, but the monarch knew very well that the expense was justified. Louisbourg was the centre of his cod fishery, a major shipping hub and a major station for privateers preying on New England, and it provided a training base for the French navy. Greater than all this was the role served by Louisbourg in guarding the gateway to New France; its position on the central east coast of Île Royale, present-day Cape Breton Island, prevented the Royal Navy from accessing the Saint Lawrence river.

Yet Pitt knew that this Gibraltar of North America was not impenetrable. In 1745, during King George's War, the fortress had been seized by British colonists supported by ships of the Royal Navy. They had managed what had been thought impossible through a siege lasting 46 days. While

Havre Louisbourg was strongly defended, the site upon which the fortress had been constructed was overlooked by a number of slight hills. These had provided excellent positions for Britain's cannons.

After the unchallenged capture, the British had held the fortress for three years until the 1748 Treaty of Aix-la-Chapelle obliged that it be returned to France. As it invariably did, Louisbourg thrived during the decade that followed. By 1758, when Pitt was calling for its capture, its garrison had grown to 3,031 men, supported by 400 militia, 2,606 marines and 10 warships. This the British countered with more than 13,000 soldiers, supported by 14,000 men on 150 Royal Navy ships and close to 2,000 mounted guns.

Charged with capturing Louisbourg was Jeffery Amherst who, having received the local rank of Major General in America, was considered commander-in-chief of the British army in North America.

The fleet sailed out of Halifax on 28 May and five days later dropped anchor in Gabarus Bay, roughly 7 km south-west of Louisbourg. Poor weather prevented his troops from going ashore until the early morning of 8 June. Their chosen landing spot, Anse de la Cormorandière, was also the most guarded; and yet the British landed, with few casualties, easily overwhelming their foe.

Once ashore, Amherst had two pineapples sent to Marie-Anne Drucour, wife of Augustin de Boschenry de Drucour, Governor of Île Royale. In return, the Major General in America received several bottles of champagne. This generosity prompted Amherst to have presented a second offering of pineapples, which was reciprocated in turn with a gift of fresh butter.

Having dispensed with such courtesies, a bombardment began from the British warships offshore.

In the early stages of the siege, rough surf prevented the British from bringing their heavy artillery ashore. Most movement by Amherst's men involved taking up positions from which, in time, they would be able to bombard the fortress.

Amherst's force was ordered in three divisions, commanded by 'Brigadiers in America' James Wolfe,

Charles Lawrence and Edward Whitmore. They gained control of the countryside with little opposition. One week later, when the British artillery batteries were finally able to land, their positions were in no way limited.

If there had been a moment of advantage for Drucour, it most certainly would have occurred during the delicate, prolonged operation in which the British carried their guns and supplies to shore through the heavy surf. And yet, the governor had failed to act.

To this point, the governor's plan had been to impede the British ships so that they would not be able to enter the Saint Lawrence before the coming of winter. However, the increased bombardment threatened this strategy. The fortification, which had still not been fully rebuilt after the siege of 1745, was beginning to fail. Despite his best efforts, and those of his wife, who had sought to inspire by herself firing three cannons each day, those inside the crumbling walls had lost hope. The situation was made worse on 21 July, when a mortar round from Wolfe's position at Pointe à la Croix set ablaze *L'Entreprenant*, a 74-gun warship. As two other French ships burned, *L'Entreprenant*, the largest in the Louisbourg fleet, exploded and sank. Two days later, another British barrage destroyed the King's Bastion, then the largest building in North America.

The end for Drucour, now close, was hastened by a thick fog which rolled in on 25 July. The British took advantage of the cover it offered and sent a cutting party to destroy the last two French ships in Havre Louisbourg. Unchallenged, the Royal Navy were then able to seize the harbour.

The next day, the governor wrote to Amherst to request terms of surrender. The response from the Major General in America was harsh: 'We give your Excellency an hour to determine on the only capitulation we are willing to grant, which is, you surrender yourselves prisoners of war.'

Recognizing that he was in no position to negotiate, Drucour accepted Amherst's terms and surrendered Louisbourg, Île Royale and Île Saint-Jean, present-day Prince Edward Island.

Those who had managed to survive the Battle of Louisbourg – Augustin and Marie-Anne Drucour included

– were deported to France. The now former governor had lost nearly all he had owned in the siege and was obliged to rely on the generosity of his brother. Destitute, he died in 1762, a little more than four years after the surrender of Louisbourg. Marie-Anne, who had worked diligently in an attempt to defend her husband's reputation, died two months later.

The Drucours' deaths had been preceded by those of all three of the 'Brigadiers in America'. In 1759, James Wolfe would die a hero's death on the Plains of Abraham, aware of his great victory over Major General Louis-Joseph de Montcalm-Gozon. The next year, Charles Lawrence would die a less noble death, cut down by a chill in his 51st year.

For a time, the future looked very bright for Edward Whitmore. Described by Wolfe as 'a poor, old, sleepy man', he was made governor of the newly rechristened Cape Breton and the Island of Saint John. His greatest responsibility in this rather relaxed, if unimportant, position was to oversee the demolition of the Fortress of Louisbourg. Once this was accomplished, he took leave so as to regain his health, boarding a ship bound for Boston. During the voyage, on 11 December 1861, he was swept overboard and drowned.

THE BATTLE *of* THE PLAINS *of* ABRAHAM

13–22 SEPTEMBER 1759

———◆———

THE BATTLE OF the Plains of Abraham is the pivotal battle in the history of Canada. Indeed, it continues to be argued that this great clash forever changed the course of two great European powers. It was the decisive event in a war which, for 19th-century historian Francis Parkman, 'made England what she is.'

As the summer of 1759 began, the war was going well for the French. Such were its fortunes that France planned to invade the British Isles, and had amassed troops near the mouth of the Loire river for just such a purpose.

However, there was a very different reality on the other side of the Atlantic Ocean. After experiencing such success in the early years of the North American war, the French were now on the defensive. They had been driven from a great number of their frontier posts, and Louisbourg, their

'Gibraltar of North America', had fallen.

In May, General James Wolfe, who had played a key role in the previous year's victory, returned to the fortress. From there he prepared the first stages of the offensive that he hoped would lead to the capture of Quebec. Wolfe led his troops inland to meet others who were advancing along Lake Champlain and still more who were coming in from points further west.

He had been expecting a combined force of some 12,000 men, but when the three prongs met their numbers disappointed. The largest body comprised 7,000 regulars, which, when combined with the roughly 400 officers, 300 gunners and a battery of Royal Marines, provided less than two-thirds of the force his plans required.

The troops were supported by a fleet of 49 ships and 140 smaller craft under the command of Admiral Charles Saunders. Before approaching Quebec, the fleet's passage was made safe by Captain James Cook, who surveyed and mapped a large portion of the easternmost Saint Lawrence river, including the hazardous Le Traverse channel. The explorer also acted as something of a pilot, helping to guide the fleet upriver.

On 28 June, Wolfe and his men arrived at Île d'Orléans, some 20 km east of Quebec. French attempts to thwart the landing by sending seven fire ships drifting downriver failed when they fired too early. British sailors were able to pull the flaming craft away from the fleet.

That day, the troops positioned themselves at Point Levis, on the south shore of the Saint Lawrence almost directly across the river from the city. Within days, a battery was established and a bombardment of Quebec's Lower Town began.

Major General Louis-Joseph de Montcalm-Gozon, Marquis of Saint-Veran, the commander of the troops, prepared for what he believed would be an assault near the small town of Beauport, 6 km to the north-east of the city. Some 12,000 French regulars and Canadian militiamen were positioned along a 9 km stretch of fortified redoubts and batteries.

Beauport itself had been planned with defence in mind.

Its stone houses were built in an unbroken line along a shoreline road. Surveying the intended site of battle, Wolfe noted that these same houses had been barricaded and readied for musket fire. None of these factors deterred him.

On 31 July, the general dispatched 3,500 troops to Beauport. Though supported by an intense barrage, the attempted landing became stalled in the river shallows. One unit, the newly formed Louisbourg Grenadiers managed to reach the shore, but drew heavy fire from French muskets. The battle came to an early end – fortunately for Wolfe – when a violent thunderstorm moved in, easing a British retreat.

By the end of the Battle of Beauport, the British had suffered 450 casualties, more than seven times the French number.

After their victory at Beauport, confidence was high within the fortified walls of Quebec. Governor Pierre François de Rigaud, Marquis de Vaudreuil-Cavagnal, wrote: 'I have no more anxiety about Quebec. Wolfe, I assure you, will make no progress.' While the governor predicted that there would be another attack within the next few days, others expressed even greater optimism. Wolfe's campaign, they asserted, had already come to an end.

Yet Wolfe remained.

Vaudreuil, too, was incorrect with his prediction. The British general did not launch another attack on Quebec; instead, he shifted his focus elsewhere. Throughout what remained of the Canadian summer, his troops sailed along the Saint Lawrence razing the small, fragile settlements of New France. It is estimated that some 1,400 French houses were destroyed in what most probably was an attempt at forcing Montcalm and his men to leave the fortifications of Quebec City. Although this event did not come to pass, the destruction benefited the British in that the amount of supplies arriving in the capital was severely reduced.

However, while the situation within the walls of Quebec was gradually edging from the inconvenient to the inhospitable, the atmosphere was much more severe in the British camps across the river. Illness spread, thinning the numbers of men ready for combat.

Wolfe, who in August had himself taken ill, began to

despair. All too aware of the coming Canadian winter, he knew that some sort of movement would have to take place before October.

In a letter to his mother, dated 31 August, Wolfe wrote of his frustration:

> *My writing to you will convince you that no personal evils worse than defeats and disappointments have fallen upon me. The enemy puts nothing to risk, and I can't in conscience put the whole army to risk. My antagonist has wisely shut himself up in inaccessible intrenchments, so that I can't get at him without spilling a torrent of blood, and that perhaps to little purpose. The Marquis de Montcalm is at the head of a great number of bad soldiers, and I am at the head of a small number of good ones, that wish for nothing so much as to fight him; but the wary old fellow avoids an action, doubtful of the behavior of his army. People must be of the profession to understand the disadvantages and difficulties we labor under, arising from the uncommon natural strength of the country.*

Wolfe had already decided that only by landing on the north shore, upriver from Quebec, would Montcalm's defensive posture be broken. Such a position would sever supply lines to Montreal, forcing the major general to leave the protection of the city. While Montcalm had stayed behind the walls of Quebec, not all of his men were with him. Nearly 3,000 were positioned about 15 km upriver at Cap-Rouge, where they kept watch on British ships. In early September, believing Wolfe's abandonment of a base camp near Beauport to have been a feint, Montcalm redeployed troops to the area.

Ultimately, the British landing site was much closer than either of these two locations. Wolfe selected Anse-aux-Foulons, a cove situated just 3 km to the south-west of the city. Situated at the foot of a 53-m cliff, protected by cannons, it was a bold choice. Other locations might have presented no natural obstacles and weaker defences, but it was Wolfe's belief that Anse-aux-Foulons was 'that spot where we can act with most force and are most likely to succeed.'

Five thousand men were involved in Wolfe's plan. All would land under cover of night. As the Anse-aux-Foulons shore consisted of nothing but a very narrow strip of land, it was essential that each landing soldier quickly moved to ascend the cliff. Having gained the high ground, the British would need to capture the garrison along with its cannons. They would then assemble for battle, hoping that Montcalm would rise to the challenge.

On the evening of 12 September, the British set out from Point Levis. For the most part, their passage went unnoticed. Canadian sentries did notice some ships, but believed them to be part of a French supply convoy that had been scheduled to pass that very night. Although this operation had been later cancelled, no one had seen fit to notify Louis Du Pont Duchambon de Vergor, captain of the local militia. When hailed, a captain from the 78th Fraser Highlanders battalion responded, managing to eliminate any suspicion. The cancelled convoy and the presence of the French-speaking Scot were just two of several lucky breaks for Wolfe's army. Earlier in the day, the governor had ordered one of the regiments out of the area and to the east of the city. That same evening, an officer charged with patrolling the cliffs found himself unable to do so after his horse was stolen.

Wolfe's luck held after the landing. His men, who proved themselves adept in scaling the cliff, found themselves at the rear of Vergor's camp. In capturing the position, one of the militiamen managed to escape. He ran for the city, where his story of the British amassing on the plains was taken as the ravings of a madman.

When dawn broke on 13 September, the truth behind the militiaman's words became all too evident. The inhabitants of Quebec awoke to discover an army of 5,000 men prepared for battle not 3 km beyond the city's fortifications.

Despite the ground gained by Wolfe, Montcalm maintained the superior position. Three thousand men commanded by his aide-de-camp, Louis-Antoine, Comte de Bougainville, were at Cap-Rouge, less than half a day's march away. Montcalm could simply await Bougainville's arrival, and then attack from the front as his aide-de-camp took the British rear. There were, of course, other options, the best of which always involved calling in the troops who were already outside the city walls. However, Montcalm chose to do exactly as Wolfe had hoped, adopting a strategy that involved leaving the fortifications behind.

That he did so without waiting for Bougainville was a mistake. Had his aide-de-camp arrived, Wolfe's force would have had no option but to retreat using the very same route which had led them to the plains: the cliff at Anse-aux-Foulons.

The British formed a line with their backs to the Saint Lawrence, and then spread out across the plains in a shallow horseshoe formation approximately 1 km in length. Its right wing was anchored to the cliffs above the Saint Lawrence, while the left wing was set in a small collection of houses they had captured. It was here that the British were first engaged. Canadian militia who had taken cover in tall grass and brush managed to retake one of the houses, setting it and several others alight. The smoke masked the left flank, quite possibly fooling Montcalm into overestimating the size of the British force.

Nevertheless, Montcalm chose to proceed with his attack. By ten o'clock, he had arrayed roughly 3,500 troops in a column formation and, mounted on his horse, ordered an advance against the British lines.

The British held their fire on Montcalm's approaching men. Following a method of Wolfe's own devising, the centre waited until the advancing force was within 20 m, before opening fire at close range. Each soldier had charged his musket with two balls, allowing their line to continue forward, and then fire a second time. This novel approach disturbed and frightened some of Montcalm's men, sending many into flight.

Early in the battle, Wolfe had been struck on the wrist, yet he continued on with his hand wrapped in cloth. Then, just after the volley that had so startled the enemy, he was struck twice, once in the stomach and then again in the chest.

Witnessing the fleeing French and Canadian troops, one soldier close to Wolfe yelled: 'They run, see how they run.' Wolfe took that to mean that the enemy had broken. After managing a few final orders, the major general turned on his side, and said 'Now, God be praised, I will die in peace,' and expired.

With Wolfe dead and his second-in-command wounded, the pursuit of the fleeing enemy became chaotic and bloody. Brigadier General George Townshend took command and was in the process of re-establishing order in the British ranks when he learned that Bougainville was approaching from the rear. In haste, two battalions were created and turned to meet the force from Cap-Rouge. Bougainville retreated, as did Montcalm and his men.

It was during this manoeuvre that the French commander was struck by what was either a piece of artillery or repeated musket fire. Suffering severe injuries to his lower abdomen, he was only just able to make it back to Quebec. With his regulars scattered and the militiamen choosing to desert, the engagement was all but over.

Montcalm's command passed to the sickly Lieutenant Jean-Baptiste-Nicolas-Roch de Ramezay, who was obliged to leave the Hôpital Général in order to serve. At a council of war held that evening at Beauport, Vaudreuil announced his decision to retreat 46 km upriver to Jacques-Cartier, and presented Ramezay with terms for the surrender of the city.

The lieutenant was instructed to give up the capital before it suffered a damaging assault. Aghast, Ramezay appealed to Montcalm to intercede, but the general was too weak to respond. He died the next morning.

Within the walls of Quebec, Ramezay was left with a force of some 2,200 men. Although the lieutenant estimated that he had eight days of rations, one day passed before representatives of the city's 4,000 inhabitants requested that he surrender Quebec. Again, Ramezay was stunned, and became even more so when 13 of his 14 senior officers recommended adopting the townspeople's request.

On 17 September, Major General Francois de Gaston, Chevalier de Lévis, arrived from Montreal at Jacques-Cartier. Meeting with Vaudreuil, a strategy was struck in which the forces would return to the city, and again engage the British on the Plains of Abraham. The governor issued new instructions to Ramezay.

Meanwhile, the situation in Quebec was worsening. Rations became tight, illness was spreading, the townspeople and Ramezay's own officers were asking for capitulation and British cannons were being assembled on the plains. Unaware of Vaudreuil's new instructions, Ramezay entered into negotiations for the surrender of the city, a process made more palatable by Townshend's acceptance of all 11 demands.

On the morning of 18 September, the Articles of Capitulation of Quebec were signed and all hostilities ceased.

Although Ramezay had managed to damage some British ships with cannon fire from within the city, the vast majority of British casualties occurred during the Battle of the Plains of Abraham. The numbers lost by both sides were similar – the British suffered 658 casualties, while 644 French and Canadians were killed or wounded.

With winter approaching, on 19 October the Royal Navy sailed out of the Saint Lawrence, leaving more than 4,000 men under the command of General James Murray.

Six months later the pack ice on the river had melted, making navigation again possible. The Chevalier de Lévis led 7,000 troops toward Quebec.

On 28 April 1760, Lévis met the British in battle at Sainte-Foy, 9 km to the south-west of the city. The Battle of Sainte-Foy was, if anything, more horrific than that which had been fought on the Plains of Abraham; nearly 2,000 men became casualties.

Defeated, with a loss of nearly one in three men, Murray withdrew to the relative safety offered by the fortifications of Quebec. Although the city was put under siege, Lévis lacked artillery and ammunition. This disadvantage, combined with improvements the British had made to their fortifications, held off the French and Canadians until the return of the Royal Navy in May. Lévis had no choice but to withdraw to Montreal.

On 8 September, confronted with 17,000 troops from Great Britain and the Thirteen Colonies, the French surrendered. The British took possession of Montreal.

Although the war continued for a further two and a half years, the fighting in North America between Great Britain and France was all but over. Weakened severely in Europe, its navy destroyed, the French were simply incapable of any attempt to retake New France.

For nearly 100 years the British and the French had fought over North America, but that struggle had now come to an end. In the century to come, the effects of the Seven Years' War would be reflected in the balance between the two powers. In his classic 1884 study, *Wolfe and Montcalm*, Francis Parkman writes of the significance the conflict had to Great Britain:

> *It crippled the commerce of her rival, ruined France in two continents, and blighted her as a colonial power. It gave England the control of the seas and the mastery of North America and India, made her the first of commercial nations, and prepared that vast colonial system that has planted new Englands in every quarter of the globe.*

CHAPTER III

---◆---

The American War *of* Independence

The WAR AGAINST REVOLUTION
1774–83

An introduction

IN OCTOBER 1774, 11 years after the end of the Seven Years' War, copies of a manifesto, written in French, were posted in the cities of Montreal and Quebec. The document was not drafted by French Canadians; rather it was the work of the First Continental Congress, a meeting of unelected delegations from all but one of the Thirteen Colonies. It was an appeal to the French Canadians to throw off British rule and 'take a noble chance for emerging from a humiliating subjection under Governors, Intendants, and Military Tyrants'. This message from the revolutionaries to the south was mixed: 'You are a small people, compared to those who with open arms invite you into a fellowship. A moment's reflection should convince you which will be most for your interest and happiness, to have all the rest of North-America your unalterable friends, or your inveterate enemies.' In this way, the document was a reflection of the position of the Thirteen Colonies towards Canada; one hand held out in invitation, the other clenched as a fist.

One reason for this confused approach is found in the Quebec Act, a British statute which had received royal assent in June 1774 and came into effect the following May. Largely the work of Governor Sir Guy Carleton, the Act increased Quebec's territory to include, among other areas, Indian country between the Ohio and Mississippi rivers to the south of the Great Lakes. The expansion angered settlers within the Thirteen Colonies who considered the land to be theirs by right. However, the issue of territory was but one of the Act's many features with which the colonies took exception. The establishment of French civil law, the maintenance of the seigneurial system and the guarantee of religious freedom for Quebec's Roman Catholic majority

– all served to fuel the growing dissatisfaction with the Crown. Indeed, the Thirteen Colonies listed the Quebec Act as one of the five 'Intolerable Acts' passed by the British Parliament.

The invitation to revolution issued by the colonies to the south failed, in part, because of its transparency. The inhabitants of Quebec were quite aware of American objections to the Act. Through their Church, French Canadians knew of the hostility to their religion. Indeed, the English-language version of the manifesto issued by the First Continental Congress included a condemnation of Catholic Canadians as being satanic. Although they possessed no great loyalty to the British Crown, French Canadians realized that the invitation from the colonies to the south was something less than trustworthy.

The American War of Independence, which had been fermenting for so very long, finally began on 19 April 1775 with the battles of Lexington and Concord. The invasion of Canada, ordered by the Continental Congress on 27 June, was the first major military initiative by the Continental army.

Violence was in no way limited to military acts. Within the Thirteen Colonies, many of those loyal to the Crown had been tarred and feathered; beatings, torture and lynching were not at all uncommon.

The war brought about the greatest migration in the history of North America; more than 100,000 people fled the Thirteen Colonies. It is believed that roughly half of the loyalists settled in British North America, most of these in Nova Scotia. Hundreds of kilometres to the west, the establishment of loyalist communities along the Detroit river, the Thames river and in the Niagara Peninsula eventually led to the creation of the Province of Upper Canada.

Their plight was mythologized and romanticized by William Kirby, himself the grandson of a loyalist in his epic poem, *The U. E.: A Tale of Upper Canada*:

> *Not drooping like poor fugitives, they came*
> *In exodus to our Canadian wilds ...*
> *King's gifts upon the exiles were bestowed.*
> *Ten thousand homes were planted; and each one*

With axe, and fire, and mutual help made war
Against the wilderness, and smote it down ...
 In the great woods content to build a home
And commonwealth, where they could live secure
A life of honour, loyalty, and peace.

THE BATTLE *of* FORT SAINT-JEAN

31 AUGUST – 3 NOVEMBER 1775

T HE BRITISH HAD many obstacles to overcome in their fight to keep the Thirteen Colonies, most of which involved geography, demographics and political structure. Stretching from Maine in the north to Georgia in the south, the colonies covered more than 360,000 square miles, making it next to impossible to maintain a military presence throughout. An added difficulty lay in the fact that more than 90 per cent of the Thirteen Colonies' 2,400,000 citizens lived inland, beyond the reach of the powerful Royal Navy. As a result, the revolution continued, despite the occupation of major American cities such as New York and Philadelphia. Finally, as 13 separate colonies joined together in a military struggle, the British faced an enemy which had no capital city. Had they been able to capture the seat of government, a traditional target in European warfare, the revolution might have turned out quite differently.

This last advantage held by the Thirteen Colonies was not one shared by the Province of Quebec. Indeed, as demonstrated during the Seven Years' War, the capture of Quebec City, the capital, virtually guaranteed the collapse of the entire colony.

The first American incursions into the Province of Quebec took place the month before the Continental Congress ordered invasion. Early in the morning of 17 May, 50 men under the command of Colonel Benedict Arnold captured a 15-man British garrison near the town of Saint-Jean-sur-Richelieu, a few kilometres inside the Province of Quebec. They destroyed five bateaux and commandeered four others, along with the sloop HMS *George III*, and set sail back south. Arnold's men had travelled roughly 20 km when they encountered a group of 60 revolutionaries known as the 'Green Mountain Boys'. Their leader, Colonel Ethan Allen, ignored Arnold's counsel and decided to seize the fort just outside of town. Located on the Richelieu river, just north of Lake Champlain, Allen and others recognized that the capture of Fort Saint-Jean, once a stronghold of the French military, would play an important part in the conquest of the province.

However, Ethan Allen's Green Mountain Boys were unprepared for such a venture, and after a brief skirmish fled back across the border.

In late August, the Continental Army launched the invasion that had been ordered by the Congress. Troops under Major General Philip Schuyler, a wealthy member of the Anglo-Dutch New York establishment, crossed into Quebec territory. In preparation to take Fort Saint-Jean, they encamped at Isle-aux-Noix, the site of another old French fort.

After the failed assault by the Green Mountain Boys, Fort Saint-Jean's garrison had been reinforced and now contained roughly 300 infantry. The skills possessed by their commander, Major Charles Preston, were second only to the Governor of Quebec, Sir Guy Carleton.

On 31 August the Continental Army attempted to storm the fort, but was turned back before reaching its walls. This failure was the first of many. Five days later, the Americans again set out from Isle-aux-Noix, landing in force 2 km from the fort. Almost immediately, they were ambushed by 100 Native Americans under the leadership of Captain Gilbert Tice, a New York loyalist. By 10 September, Schuyler had regrouped and was leading a force of more than 800 towards the fort, when a failure of nerve broke out among his men. Fearing an ambush like the one suffered a few days earlier, many simply broke and ran off. The major general had no alternative but to retreat to the Isle-aux-Noix camp without even having encountered the enemy.

After these failures, Schuyler, at best an unpopular leader, withdrew from the effort, professing gout and rheumatism as the cause. He was replaced by Richard Montgomery, an Irish immigrant who had settled in New York.

The Americans changed their tactics and laid siege to Fort Saint-Jean through the use of a force which would eventually include 2,500 regulars. The fort was subjected to a constant bombardment. As the conditions within deteriorated, Preston requested reinforcements from Carleton. However, the governor had few men to spare. Refusing Preston's request,

Carleton held on to his small force at Montreal, which consisted of only 35 regulars. His fears that the colony's second largest city would come under attack proved justified when on the evening of 24 September the regulars fought off an assault by more than 100 revolutionaries. Another of Allen's ill-fated expeditions, the brief battle served to mobilize the militia. As many as 2,000 men were assembled, but this number was short-lived; most were soon on their way home to attend to the autumn harvest.

For the Americans, the Battle of Longue Point, as it became known, amounted to little more than a setback. During the night of 17 October, when the siege of Fort Saint-Jean was in its sixth week, Montgomery's men managed to slip several 9-lb (4-kg) cannons past the stronghold. They were sailed 14 km downriver where they were used to attack Fort Chambly. Within 24 hours, this smaller British outpost had fallen; Preston and his men were now completely cut off.

Although Preston held out for as long as possible, on 3 November, with winter setting in and provisions running low, Fort Saint-Jean was surrendered to Montgomery. In the nine weeks that had elapsed between the first Continental Army assault on the fort and its surrender, the major had lost 40 men. The American casualties were much greater. More than 100 had been killed or wounded at the hands of the British and Canadians; a further 900 had been lost to illness.

The Battle of Fort Saint-Jean lacked great action and drama, yet had grave consequences for the Province of Quebec. With the stronghold having been removed as an obstacle, the American revolutionaries were free to advance north. Ten days later, Carleton ordered that Montreal be evacuated and, intent on protecting the capital, moved his small force on to Quebec City. Within hours, Montgomery entered through the Récollet Gate.

Although Preston had lost Fort Saint-Jean, his defiance had prolonged a siege that had been expected to last no longer than a few weeks. In doing so, Preston delayed the planned assault on Quebec City, thereby ensuring that the revolutionaries would have to overcome the hardships of a Quebec winter.

THE BATTLE *of* QUEBEC
31 DECEMBER 1775

———•———

BRIGADIER GENERAL Richard Montgomery's move up Lake Champlain and the Richelieu river was part of what was intended as a two-columned attack on the capital of Quebec. In September 1775, not long after the siege of Fort Saint-Jean had begun, nearly 1,100 troops under the command of Colonel Benedict Arnold marched from Cambridge, Massachusetts to the mouth of the Merrimac river, where they boarded ships bound for Maine. The route they were following was one that had once been used by the French. Not nearly as straightforward as that offered Montgomery, it involved the Kennebec river, the Dead river, Lake Megantic, the Chaudière river and a number of overland marches which, together, would bring the Continental Army to the south shore of the Saint Lawrence river, opposite Quebec City.

Promoted by George Washington, Arnold's course was

much more difficult and more than twice as long as the future American president had suggested. It took the column more than six weeks to reach Quebec's capital. Fighting rapids in the autumn rain and wading through frigid waters, the men were forced to rely on a diet consisting of boiled shoe leather, moss, cartridge boxes and tree bark. Arnold ate his pet Newfoundland dog. Beleaguered by disenchantment and illness, by 8 November, the day Arnold finally reached the Saint Lawrence, more than 500 of his 1,100 men had been lost through death and desertion. Even the Saint Lawrence proved to be a problem. The column spent several days trying to shelter themselves from a vicious gale before they were finally able to cross to the river.

Arnold had his men encamp on the battleground of Wolfe and Montcalm, the Plains of Abraham. There the brigadier general laid siege to what he surely recognized as a well-stocked, walled city. Within those city walls rested a force of 1,200 men, more than twice the number of Arnold's army, and yet the American brigadier general felt confident. In a letter to Hector Cramahé, assistant to Sir Guy Carleton, he made a bold demand: 'I am ordered by his excellency Gen. Washington to take possession of the town of Quebec. I do therefore, in the name of the United Colonies, demand immediate surrender of the town, fortifications & c. of Quebec to the forces of the United Colonies under my command'.

Neither Cramahé nor Carleton chose to acknowledge Arnold's letter. While Arnold awaited a response that would never come, Montgomery was securing Montreal. On 28 November, he left the city under the command of General David Wooster and with most of his men proceeded to Quebec. After having been delayed during their siege at Fort Saint-Jean, Montgomery's column was now making good speed. It took the force just five days to reach the capital city.

Montgomery, too, addressed a letter to the governor, which Carleton burned unread.

The Continental Army's siege had little effect on a city that had prepared itself for winter. The commanders saw that Carleton was content to remain within the comfort and protection offered by the city, while their own men suffered out in the open, under blankets, as temperatures dropped. As the weeks passed, their numbers decreasing due to desertion, pneumonia and smallpox, Arnold and Montgomery knew that a full assault on the city was required. They determined that their best chance of success would come under cover of a winter storm. And yet, to their frustration, the skies remained clear.

With the New Year approaching, the two commanders had an additional pressure; their enlisted men were obliged to serve only until 31 December. Arnold and Montgomery knew full well that once released from their obligations, almost all under their command would immediately return to their homes.

Fortune shone down on the two men when, on 30 December, the blizzard for which they had hoped finally arrived. Initial sign of attack began in the early hours of the next morning, when Montgomery sent up two signal rockets, barely visible through the falling snow.

In launching their end-of-year attack, Montgomery and Arnold chose to ignore Quebec's impenetrable, walled

Upper Town, protected by the Citadel, and concentrated only on the Lower Town. The plan called for Montgomery to attack from the south-west, while Arnold would advance from the eastern side. Nothing in this strategy came as a surprise to Carleton who, unknown to the revolutionaries, had fortified both points.

Montgomery's brigade hugged the narrow shoreline, advancing on the Lower Town under the Cape Diamond Bastion, until they came upon a blockhouse at Près-de-Ville. It was manned by about 30 French Canadian militiamen who, alert and at the ready, watched as the revolutionaries charged forward. Just as Montgomery made the brash declaration, 'Quebec is ours!', a single volley of grapeshot was fired from the blockhouse. The general was hit in the head and, one presumes, died instantly. The next two highest ranking officers were also killed, leaving the fourth ranking officer to order a retreat. Other members of the dead commander's brigade were cut down by musket balls as they fled.

Unaware of Montgomery's death, Arnold and his brigade

of 700 men advanced in the north-west, beneath Quebec's steep bluff and city walls. Their actions were watched by the local militia stationed in the Upper Town, who let loose a shower of musket balls on to the revolutionaries below. Arnold was wounded in the left ankle, and had to be carried to the rear. It fell to his second-in-command, Daniel Morgan, to lead the brigade forward to the point of their planned rendezvous with Montgomery and his men. However, once achieving this position, Morgan did nothing but wait for a brigade that had already retreated. He was soon attacked by a large group of militia led by Carleton. The narrow streets of the old part of town rendered retreat impossible. At nine o'clock in the morning, just hours after Montgomery had launched his signal rockets, Morgan surrendered; the Battle of Quebec had come to an end.

In reporting the battle, Carleton recorded the deaths of one British naval officer and five French Canadian militiamen; those wounded amounted to four British regulars and 15 of the militia. The casualties among members of the Continental Army are somewhat less precise. At least

42 revolutionaries were killed, though the correct number may be significantly higher. It is thought that many drowned while attempting to flee across the frozen Saint Lawrence river. More than 400 of the invading revolutionaries were wounded.

The body of Richard Montgomery was discovered the next day, but only because its hand was visible, sticking out of the freshly fallen snow. The remains of some 20 other Americans were revealed with the melting of the snow the following spring.

Despite the clear defeat and depleted force, Arnold's confidence remained high. While recovering from his wound, he wrote to his wife: 'I have no thoughts of leaving this proud town until I first enter it in triumph.' Arnold refused to withdraw, but during the early months of 1776 he struggled to maintain his ineffective siege of Quebec. In March, the arrival of reinforcements increased his force to 2,000 men. Still, his presence outside the city walls had little effect. His work to stage a second assault on the city amounted to nothing.

In April, Arnold left Quebec for Montreal, which he presumed would be a city more receptive to the revolution. He left Major General John Thomas in charge of a siege which would soon come to an end. In early May, the ice on the Saint Lawrence having broken up, three Royal Navy ships carrying reinforcements landed at Quebec's capital. Thomas and his men withdrew, abandoning muskets, artillery and more than 200 soldiers of the Continental Army who, suffering from dysentery and smallpox, were too ill to join the retreat.

The Battle *of* Trois-Rivières
8 June 1776

BEFORE THE SIEGE of Saint-Jean, the occupation of Montreal and the Battle of Quebec, the revolutionaries had enjoyed a considerable degree of support within the mother country. A significant percentage of the population understood and sympathized with the American grievances outlined in the 'Intolerable Acts'. Anti-war sentiment had been particularly strong among the commercial classes, who benefited greatly from trade with the colonies. However, the 1775 invasion of the Province of Quebec brought about a substantial shift in public sentiment. No longer were the revolutionaries considered as colonials protesting against injustices, but insurgents who were intent on exporting a revolution through violence and destruction.

In Montreal, which was still under occupation, public opinion had also swung against the revolutionaries.

Originally of neutral opinion, most had ignored Governor Sir Guy Carleton's 13 November evacuation order. When the revolutionary General Richard Montgomery led his force of occupation into the city, several prominent citizens had welcomed him with a document in which they declared: 'Our chains are broken, blissful liberty restores us to ourselves'. Montgomery, in turn, promised 'liberty and security', but the assurance had not met expectations.

Within weeks, many Montrealers suspected of being less than supportive of the revolution were rounded up and imprisoned at Fort Chambly. Anti-Catholic sentiment, which was rampant among the occupying force, led to the banning of Christmas mass and the closing of churches. Lacking provisions, the revolutionaries began looting farms and homes.

On 29 April, a small contingent of representatives arrived in Montreal, charged by the Continental Congress with propagating support for the revolution. Benjamin Franklin, the leader of this three-man group, found a city that had become openly hostile to the Americans. It had taken

Franklin a month to make the journey from his Philadelphia home to Montreal – 12 days later he was on his way back. The 'miserable situation', as he described it, was hopeless.

Yet, Benedict Arnold – now a brigadier general – stayed on, ever confident that the Province of Quebec could be won. His faith remained even after the 6 May arrival of Royal Navy ships in the harbour at Quebec City. The British reinforcements to land, carried by the fittingly named HMS *Surprise*, were the first of an eventual 13,000. Wishing to assemble the full force, Carleton had chosen not to pursue American General John Thomas and his men when they abandoned their siege on Quebec City.

With a force of roughly 250, Thomas withdrew up the Saint Lawrence river to the mouth of the Richelieu river, before he died of smallpox, the disease that had claimed so many of his men on the Plains of Abraham. His replacement, General John Sullivan, was determined to turn the location – present-day Sorel – into a base for the Continental Army.

What Sullivan did not realize was that two great changes had taken place since the Continental Congress had ordered the invasion one year earlier. Where once the French Canadians had been largely indifferent to the revolutionaries from the south, events at Fort Saint-Jean and Montreal had led to support for the Crown. While this change in attitude was significant, the consequences were less immediate than was the difference in force under Carleton's command. The regulars carried by the Royal Navy ships arriving at Quebec City had increased his standing army more than 30-fold.

In June, Carleton began moving 3,000 men towards Sullivan's force of 2,500. Sullivan moved to meet them downriver at Trois-Rivières in what was intended to be a surprise attack. At the start, Sullivan fell victim to the anti-revolutionary sentiment that had taken root in the colony. A Canadian guide led his men intentionally away from their enemy. After this betrayal was discovered, they became lost trying to retrace their steps. At dawn, Sullivan's force was spotted and fired upon by British vessels on the river. In running for cover the revolutionaries became separated.

After a couple of hours of chaos, several hundred men led by William Thompson, the largest of the army's scattered groups, were confronted by a line of entrenched British regulars under General John Burgoyne.

Thompson's brigade charged, then quickly withdrew under heavy fire only to find their retreat was blocked by another line of British regulars. However, Carleton had provided a route out, allowing them to escape to the Richelieu. Nevertheless, 236 soldiers of the Continental Army chose to surrender, rather than risk further combat, ambush and starvation.

Later, when questioned about his decision by one of his officers, Carleton responded: 'What would you do with them? Have you spare provisions for them? Or would you send them to Quebec to starve? No, let the poor creatures go home and carry with them a tale which will serve his majesty more effectually than their capture.'

The Battle of Trois-Rivières marked the end of the Continental Army's attempt to capture the Province of Quebec, a reality recognized even by the ever-confident Benedict Arnold. On the outskirts of Montreal, 100 km south-west, the brigadier general had suffered his own defeats

– at the Battle of the Cedars and the Battle of Vaudreuil – leading to a loss of more than 500 men. No longer able to control the region, and with Montreal growing increasingly hostile, on 15 June he attempted to set the city ablaze. Arnold and his men retreated up the Richelieu river and into Lake Champlain, the very same route Montgomery's column had employed in reverse the previous autumn.

Writing to Sullivan, Arnold argued that they must return to 'secure our own country before it is too late.' Although Arnold achieved no success in the Province of Quebec, his participation in the early stages of the American War of Independence was otherwise accomplished. Ultimately, all was overshadowed when in 1780 he turned traitor, offering to surrender West Point in exchange for £20,000. Arnold lived for five years in New Brunswick after the war and in 1798 was awarded a substantial land grant in Upper Canada. He died in London, England, three years later.

The month after the Continental Army withdrew from the Province of Quebec, the Continental Congress issued the

Declaration of Independence. Their desire to capture the colony to the north did not diminish. Late in 1777, the young country's Board of War began work on a new approach which would involve their new alliance with France. In fact, under the Marquis de Lafayette, the French were charged with leading the campaign. Ultimately, the planning came to nothing. As Lafayette made his way towards the border, he discovered that few preparations had been made. He was informed by scouts that the British and Canadians were well aware of the new plans for invasion and were standing ready in wait. Faced with certain defeat, Lafayette and the Board of War abandoned the plan. A few minor skirmishes aside, British North America remained untouched during the remaining six years of the war.

CHAPTER IV

—◆—

The War *of* 1812

The
Fight
for
Survival
1812–14

An introduction

THE GREATEST CONFLICT to be fought on Canadian soil, the War of 1812 is known by many names. When mentioned in British texts, it is more often than not referred to as 'The British-American War'. In the United States, where it was once known as 'The Second War of Independence', the struggle has come to be dubbed 'The Forgotten War'. It is an appropriate label; two centuries later this brutal war seems fairly buried by the nations involved. Even in Canada, the site of much of the bloodiest fighting, the conflict is all but a ghost, the presence of which is maintained, in the main, through a chain of sweet shops named Laura Secord, after the war's greatest heroine.

The roots of the conflict stretch back to the American War of Independence. Though the Treaty of Paris had officially ended the hostilities, tensions between Britain and the United States remained, rising and falling during the decades that followed. Several states refused to restore confiscated loyalist property, Virginia maintained wartime laws enacted against payment of debts to British creditors and true geography proved not to match the details given in boundary descriptions. The greatest area of worry was centred on the Great Lakes, which the British had held as part of an effort to obtain compensation for debts and confiscated loyalist property. A decade later, this violation of the Treaty of Paris was abandoned due, partially, to the more pressing requirements of the French Revolutionary Wars. The hostilities ended with the signing of the Treaty of Amiens on 25 March 1802, but within 14 months France and Great Britain were again at war.

It was during this second conflict, considered the first of the Napoleonic Wars, that unsteady relations between

Great Britain and the United States began to truly tilt.

Napoleon's Berlin Decree, which forbade British goods from being imported into allied countries, was countered by a similar order from Westminster. The blockade of ports in continental Europe, combined with the seizure of American ships, led to a number of ineffective retaliatory Acts passed by the United States.

Trade was further disrupted when the Royal Navy undertook a policy of impressments, and began boarding American merchant ships in order to reclaim seamen. The measure was targeted on British subjects, yet an estimated 6,000 Americans were swept up in the effort and forced to serve in the fight against the French. Many were former British subjects whom the Crown would not recognize as naturalized citizens of the United States. Relations deteriorated further in 1807 when HMS *Leopard*, fired upon, then boarded USS *Chesapeake*. Three men were killed and 18 were injured. The British boarding party discovered four deserters from the Royal Navy, one of whom was later hanged.

'The *Chesapeake* Affair', the blockades, the seizure of ships and the policy of impressments, combined with a growing desire to bring British North America into the union through annexation, prompted calls for war within the House of Representatives. Led by the 'War Hawks' – the first group to be so dubbed – the United States Congress voted in support of war against Great Britain. Following a similar vote in the Senate, President James Madison signed the measure on 18 June; it marked the first time the United States had declared war on another nation.

In New England, support for the war was tepid at best. These states valued greatly their trade with Great Britain, and would gain nothing in territorial expansion. The reluctance of Maine's militia to attack British North America meant that New Brunswick, Prince Edward Island, Nova Scotia and Newfoundland had little participation in the conflict.

Though the United States was officially at war with Great Britain, considerably more than half of the British forces were composed of Canadians. The war was fought on the

Atlantic, the Pacific, the coast of the Gulf of Mexico, and in the eastern and central regions of North America. The green and pleasant land of England – indeed, all of the United Kingdom – remained unscathed.

THE BATTLE *of* FORT DETROIT
15–16 AUGUST 1812

———•———

THE UNITED STATES was unprepared for war, despite years of growing clamour from the War Hawks. The nation's military consisted of fewer than 8,000 regulars, almost all of whom were under the command of elderly veterans of the American War of Independence. There was little support from militias, who under law were not obliged to serve beyond the boundaries of their home states. The single greatest advantage the Americans had lay in events overseas, where the United Kingdom was engaged heavily in the Napoleonic Wars. This is not to say that there was no military presence in Britain's remaining North American colonies. An official report created at the beginning of the war put the level of troops at 5,004, the majority of whom were Canadian.

The earliest victory, little more than a trivial footnote, was American. On 23 June, five days after the formal declaration of war, a British frigate was forced to discard its cargo in order to evade USS *Hornet*, a sloop-of-war. The incident was followed by the 2 July capture of the American schooner *Cuyahoga* as it sailed up the Detroit river from Lake Erie. With only a few dozen sickly soldiers on board, it at first appeared a minor accomplishment. However, it was soon discovered that the ship was also carrying the journals and correspondence of General William Hull. The Governor of Michigan, Hull was at that moment marching a force of 2,500 men towards Fort Detroit, from which he intended to launch an invasion into Upper Canada.

Hull arrived at Fort Detroit three days later and, upon learning of the seizure, sent an envoy under flag of truce to ask that the papers be returned. This request was politely denied, the commanding officer explaining that higher authorization was required.

Hull's papers merely confirmed a strategy that the British had already construed. The general proceeded very much according to plan. On 12 July, he and his men crossed the Detroit river into Upper Canada at Sandwich, in present-day

Windsor. Recognizing that the Americans outnumbered the Upper Canadians by a factor of more than 16 to 1, Major General Isaac Brock, the lieutenant governor and commander of forces, chose not to confront Hull. The American general took the finest of Sandwich's Georgian homes for his headquarters, from which he issued a proclamation in which he declared his intentions to protect and liberate the 'Inhabitants of Canada' from the 'tyranny and oppression' of Great Britain: 'The United States offer you peace, liberty and security. Your choice lies between these and war, slavery and destruction. Choose then, but choose wisely; and may HE, who knows the justice of our cause, and who holds in HIS hand the fate of Nations, guide you to a result the most compatible with your rights and interests, your peace and prosperity.' This curious document, both threatening and welcoming, reflects the bold presumption made by so very many supporters of the war, that Canadians would readily join the union to the south. Indeed, Thomas Jefferson, President Madison's precursor, described the conquest of Canada as 'a mere matter of marching'. The goodwill, if any, present among Canadian citizens, was rapidly destroyed by the plundering and looting of the self-proclaimed liberators as they advanced.

Meanwhile, slightly more than 400 km away, British and Native American forces captured Michigan's Fort Mackinac. Not a shot had been fired; unaware that war had been declared, the outnumbered American regulars had simply surrendered. The news shook Hull, who had been extremely fearful of First Nations participation in the struggle. In fact, in his proclamation the general had warned: 'The first stroke of a tomahawk, the first attempt with the scalping-knife, will be the signal for one indiscriminate scene of desolation. *No white man found fighting by the side of an Indian will be taken prisoner.* Instant destruction will be his lot.'

In Hull's words, participation of the Native Americans at Fort Mackinac was 'the opening of the hive'. His advance ground to a halt as he was overcome by indecision. On 11 August, Hull ordered his men back to Fort Detroit. In the 30 days of their occupation they had accomplished nothing, save the furthering of resentment among the citizens of Upper Canada.

Brock, too, was on the move. He had left his headquarters in York, now Toronto, for the Niagara frontier. Here, he attempted to gauge the threat posed by the Americans. The loss of the frontier, Brock recognized, would most certainly bring about the collapse of all Canadian territory to the west of Lake Ontario. On 5 August, he and a militia of 300 set out by mixed flotilla for Fort Malden, the British military facility closest to Fort Detroit. It was there that Brock met Tecumseh, the man who would become his greatest ally in the fight against the Americans.

A Shawnee, Tecumseh had devoted his life to preservation of the Native American way of life and the protection of land from American encroachment. Having built a loose confederacy of tribes, in 1811 Tecumseh went to war with the United States, a conflict which was still ongoing. In allying his confederacy with the British, the leader saw an opportunity to realize a Native American homeland in the west.

In the American Hull, Brock saw a timid, indecisive man. More than this, the British major general recognized his opponent to be extremely fearful of Native Americans.

With Tecumseh by his side, he chose to play this fear to his advantage.

Over the course of two days he risked moving all available men into position at Sandwich. His goal, the capture of Fort Detroit on the opposite side of the river, was bold in the extreme. Hull sat in wait on higher ground, in a heavily fortified position, supported by field guns and more than 2,000 infantry and cavalry. Brock's force consisted of 300 regulars, 400 inexperienced militia and 600 of Tecumseh's warriors. His artillery, small in number, was supported by the guns of the *Queen Charlotte*, a Provincial Marine vessel.

As Hull had, when requesting his documents seven weeks earlier, Brock dispensed two aides under flag of truce. In the message delivered, the general called for the surrender of Fort Detroit, and spoke of concerns that he might not be able to control his Native American warriors in the event of an assault. Hull refused to cede.

As evening fell, British artillery opened fire on the American fort. Under cover of darkness, Tecumseh and his warriors crossed the river, and secured a landing to the south of the fort. Brock remained behind, gathering all the men he could muster and clothing them in the cast-offs of regulars. When he crossed with his men at dawn, Brock's infantry appeared much greater than borne out by reality. Riding with Tecumseh, he led his men to the fort, where they arrayed in three columns. The Native American warriors moved into position through the surrounding woods, where they remained so as to hide their numbers. At Tecumseh's command, they screeched and yelled, taking advantage of Hull's fear of a massacre at the hands of the 'savages'. Before a single shot was fired, the American general raised a white flag, surrendering the fort to the British.

The Battle of Fort Detroit was the first major victory of the War of 1812, and yet no lives had been lost. Despite hours of cannon fire, no one had been killed. The defeat for the Americans was significant. Hull and nearly 600 regulars were taken prisoner and sent to Quebec, while 1,600 Ohio militiamen were paroled and sent home. Brock not only had the fort, but its horses, stores, artillery, ammunition and thousands of guns. Hull also surrendered the *Adams*, a 200-

ton (181-tonne) brig. Renamed HMS *Detroit*, it took its place beside HMS *Queen Charlotte*, giving the British undisputed control of Lake Erie.

THE BATTLE *of* QUEENSTON HEIGHTS

3 OCTOBER 1812

GENERAL WILLIAM HULL's invasion and brief occupation of the southernmost part of Upper Canada, laid to rest in the Battle of Fort Detroit, was part of an effort to divert British attention and troops to the west, away from Montreal and Quebec. Indeed, the person in command of the United States' north-east sector, Major General Henry Dearborn, a former Secretary of War, ordered his troops to Plattsburg, Vermont from which he intended to invade Lower Canada.

The second assault to the west was to take place some 400 km from Fort Detroit on the Niagara frontier. The American commander, Stephen Van Rensselaer, though a major general in the New York militia, was anything but a military man. He had achieved the position through state governor Daniel Tompkins, who saw an appointment as a means of removing a rival from the political sphere. Dearborn, who most certainly recognized Van Rensselaer's inexperience, dispatched Virginian Brigadier General Alexander Smyth to New York State, providing but vague instructions on the sharing of command. Therefore, there were no British or Canadians involved in the initial conflict; the fighting was between Van Rensselaer and Smyth.

As Smyth refused so much as to meet with Van Rensselaer, the battle was waged through correspondence. Neither man could agree on who would lead or where the attack would occur. Van Rensselaer had determined Queenston Heights as the best place to land, and so had moved his troops to Lewiston on the opposite shore. Smyth argued that a more effective landing could be made across from Buffalo, and refused to move the 1,700 men under his command. It was true that at this point the Canadian shore was more hospitable for such a campaign, but this fact had been recognized by the British, who had positioned a great number of troops in the area.

The hostile exchange between the two commanders lasted for several days. President Madison, though aware of the stalemate, did nothing. Dearborn, who seemed content in his Albany office, forever planning, wrote to Van Rensselaer and Smyth to say that their bickering was 'regrettable'.

From the Canadian side of the Niagara, Major General Isaac Brock and other officers recognized a gathering American force. Though their resources were thin, they intended to meet the invaders head on. The reception would be the opposite of that which had met Hull two months earlier. Brock believed a British victory would be decisive. 'I do not imagine the gentry from the other side will be anxious to return to the charge', he wrote to his brother. On the other hand, a loss would mean 'the province is inevitably gone'.

Meanwhile, as the stalemate between Smyth and Van Rensselaer dragged on, the latter began to fear that the situation was all part of a complex game driven by his political enemies. Van Rensselaer decided to proceed without the Virginian and his troops. In the early hours of

11 October, he ordered his men across the Niagara river. A comical mess ensued. The same clouds that added to the darkness of the night rained down on the troops as they made their way to the boats. Carts became stuck in the mud, prompting shouts which served to alert the British and Canadians stationed across the river. One of the bateaux had been swept downstream, taking the boat officer and all oars for the other craft with it. He was discovered two hours later after the bateaux had become grounded on a sandbar. In the end, Van Rensselaer was forced to call off the attack. Not one of his men had managed to reach the Canadian shore, a mere 200 m away.

The invasion had been botched to such an extent that Brock, for one, thought it must have been a ruse. As a result, he became convinced that Fort George, 10 km to the north, would be the true site of a planned invasion; no more troops would be allocated for Queenston.

At approximately three o'clock on the morning of 13 October, Van Rensselaer tried again. The first assault wave, numbering 600 men, left the Lewiston ferry landing.

Overloaded with troops, the first three boats were swept downstream under fire from 46 regulars and a few militiamen on the Canadian side. The Americans lost 200 men before their boats reached the shore. Among the first to land was Lieutenant Colonel Solomon Van Rensselaer, second cousin and aide-de-camp of the major general. He was taken down immediately – six musket balls struck his legs.

At Fort George, Brock had been awoken by cannon fire from the south. His men were roused and told to march towards the enemy which, he presumed, must have landed at Queenston Heights. Brock rode ahead along the muddy wagon trail towards Queenston, arriving in the town at dawn, just in time to see a second American wave setting out from Lewiston.

While most of Van Rensselaer's men remained at the beachhead, unable to scale the heights, an American infantry officer, Captain John Wool, had discovered a narrow fishermen's path to the summit. Hidden by trees and other vegetation, he led approximately 200 American troops up to the plateau, where they advanced through the surrounding woods. They emerged in a sudden charge, quickly seizing the battery as the few British gunners fled to the village for safety.

It was there, in Queenston itself, that Brock began to organize the troops present. He could not wait for the reinforcements from Fort George, determining a swift counter-attack would prevent Wool and his men from securing position.

Leading the charge towards the American line, Brock was an obvious target; his plumed hat, gold and epaulettes, together with a scarf given him by Tecumseh, set him apart from the several dozen other men. He was struck on the wrist, yet carried on, before being pushed back by the Americans. Brock rallied his men and had started a second charge towards the summit when a musket ball caught him just above the heart. He died within seconds.

Brock's troops fell back, but were intercepted by Lieutenant Colonel John Macdonell and a handful of York Volunteers. To the cry of 'Revenge the General', he led the men back towards the plateau. Macdonell, too, was cut down, mortally wounded by a scout's musket ball and subsequent fall from his horse.

The 70 or so British and Canadians could not meet the challenge posed by the hundreds of Americans now gathered on the summit. Carrying the dying Macdonell and the body of Brock, the British and Canadians retreated to a farm 1 km north of the village.

Boats continued to ferry American soldiers across the river; however, it wasn't until noon that Major General Van Rensselaer himself arrived at Queenston Heights. His time on the Canadian side was brief. After a quick assessment of the situation, Van Rensselaer ordered the American position to be fortified, and returned to the American shore. With his cousin now unconscious and Wool badly wounded, the major general left in command two men: Colonel Winfield Scott, who took charge of the regulars, and Brigadier General William Wadsworth, who would lead the militiamen. Together, Scott and Wadsworth commanded more than 1,000 men. However, most units were incomplete; unaware that Brock was dead, and not recognizing that the capture of the battery virtually guaranteed safe passage, hundreds of militiamen remained in Lewiston, refusing to cross the Niagara.

Van Rensselaer's departure from Queenston Heights very nearly coincided with the arrival of the first regulars from Fort George. They moved unchallenged into the village, where they set up two 6-lb (2.5-kg) guns. By one o'clock, cannon volleys were again raining down on the Niagara river; the short passage to Upper Canada had again become deadly.

The reinforcements from Fort George were soon joined by Mohawk warriors under captains John Brant and John Norton. Their war cries echoed throughout Queenston Heights and carried across the river, playing on the American fears of Native Americans. At Lewiston, Van Rensselaer appeared to have given up. Unbeknown to the British and Canadians, or even those American troops in Queenston Heights, he had begun organizing a withdrawal. However, all his efforts were unsuccessful; no boatman wanted to risk the passage to the Canadian side.

Lacking reinforcements, and with no means of retreat, the American troops were stuck.

At two o'clock, Major General Roger Hale Sheaffe, formerly Brock's second-in-command, arrived at Queenston. Taking charge, he led the troops on a 5-km march around the Heights. There he was joined by a column of reinforcements, led by Captain Richard Bullock, coming in from Chippewa. This brought the number of British and Canadian soldiers to more than 800 men. While Scott and Wadsworth's men still outnumbered the British and Canadians, their advantage had narrowed considerably. When Sheaffe attacked, the militiamen abandoned their positions, leaving the regulars to go it alone. Scott attempted an organized withdrawal by ordering his men to the river. Though the men were clearly visible from the American shore, still no boats arrived; Scott was forced to surrender.

The defeat further shook American confidence. No longer was it assumed that the conquest of Canada would be 'a mere matter of marching'. Stephen Van Rensselaer resigned his position, only to be replaced by Alexander Smyth, whose refusal to support the assault had contributed greatly to the American loss. He proved himself equally inept. After the defeats at Fort Detroit and Queenston Heights, Henry Dearborn chose not to strike at Montreal, the assault he himself had intended to command.

The Battle of Queenston Heights remains one of the largest fought on Canadian soil. It was a decisive victory for British and Canadian forces: more than 100 American lives were lost, approximately 500 were injured and nearly 1,000 were taken prisoner. The figures stood in stark contrast with those of the British and Canadians, who had suffered only 96 casualties. Ultimately, however, their great achievement was overshadowed by the fact that Sir Isaac Brock lay among their 14 dead.

THE BATTLE *of* FRENCHTOWN
22 JANUARY 1813

―――•―――

IN HIS FAILED attempt to rally the regulars at the Battle of Queenston Heights, Colonel Scott had urged his men to redeem the honour lost at Fort Detroit. William Hull's surrender weighed heavily on the United States, which, with winter descending, saw little opportunity to rid the British and Canadians from American soil. The Michigan Territory had been lost and much of Indiana Territory and Ohio were now under enemy control. Conversely, the only American forces in British North America were prisoners of war, held hundreds of kilometres from where they had been captured. To many in the southern republic, it seemed incredible that the British colonies to the north, with a combined population of 300,000, had proven themselves superior in battle to a united nation of some 8,000,000.

Among those being held by the British and Canadians was Hull himself, who had been taken into custody at the conclusion of the Battle of Fort Detroit. He was replaced by General William Henry Harrison. The self-possessed and ambitious Governor of the Indiana Territory, Harrison had won the command of the Army of the Northwest over his rival, General James Winchester. Harrison's victory had been predetermined. In 1811, he had gained national celebrity for leading American forces against Tecumseh's Native American confederacy at the Battle of Tippecanoe in the Indiana Territory. Winchester, like Hull, was a veteran of the American War of Independence. Beside the younger, dashing Harrison, he appeared tired and ponderous.

Taking charge of the army at Cincinnati, Harrison split his force into two columns, one of which he would lead personally. The other column was placed in the command of Winchester. Through the autumn of 1812, the generals moved their men north, searching out and destroying Native American tribes who, Harrison was convinced, were without exception in league with the British. Casualties on both sides were high, though this did not prevent the younger general from reporting overwhelming success. The claims were similar to those that had brought him fame. Anything but a great victory, hard-won against a significant foe, the Battle of Tippecanoe had in fact been a minor, indecisive skirmish; Harrison's losses far exceeded those of the enemy.

As 1812 drew to a close and the army progressed northwards, Harrison turned his attention away from the Native Americans and towards the British; he became intent on taking back Fort Detroit.

Though it had been part of Harrison's strategy that Winchester's column support his own, the veteran of the revolution had over time moved far in advance. By early January 1813, he and his men had reached the Maumee river, just south of the Michigan Territory. None of this had escaped the notice of Lieutenant Colonel Henry Procter, the commander of British and Canadian troops on the western front. Having been made aware by Native American scouts of Winchester's movements to the south, Procter called out the militia and requested that Tecumseh's warriors be assembled. All were intended to scorch the earth along the Detroit frontier; the Americans would be denied shelter and provisions. On 14 January 1813, Major Ebenezer Reynolds of the Essex militia, two flank companies and a group of Potawatomi warriors set out to raze Frenchtown, a village of 20 or so structures on the north shore of the River Raisin.

Winchester, who was waiting for Harrison's column at the rapids of Maumee, was faced with a dilemma; should he remain or come to the aid of the inhabitants of Frenchtown? The decision was an easy one. Winchester had been told that the Canadians numbered in the dozens and were supported by no more than 100 warriors. His column greatly outnumbered the enemy in Frenchtown. Urged on by his most popular man, Lieutenant Colonel John Allen, Winchester foresaw an easy victory, one which would restore confidence in the war and establish himself as a hero.

Allen and 100 troops were sent with a force of 450 under the command of Lieutenant Colonel William Lewis to attack the enemy at Frenchtown. On the morning of 18 January, the Americans marched until they came within sight of the village. Their first challenge, coming in the form of a small cannon, did nothing to impede progress. The Americans crossed the frozen Raisin, charging into Frenchtown. Overwhelmed, the Canadians and Native American warriors were forced back into the forest. Fighting continued until dark, by which point the Americans had succeeded in pushing their enemy back 3 km from the village.

News of the success further emboldened Winchester, leading him to order a further 300 men to Frenchtown. On 20 January, more than 48 hours after the fighting had ceased, the general himself arrived in the village. He was met by weary soldiers, many of them drunk, who had neither concern nor interest in entrenching their position. Even Winchester appeared unconcerned about the enemy – this despite the fact that the nearest British fort was only 24 km away. As his men settled into the village of Frenchtown, the general moved to the opposite side of the river, taking up residence in the largest house in the area. Winchester was bolstered further by the news that Harrison's column had arrived at the Maumee rapids.

Winchester's confidence was such that a report of approaching British soldiers and Native American warriors was not taken seriously. Another account, in which a tavern keeper had overheard a conversation between two British officers discussing an impending attack, was ignored.

Then, in the early hours of 22 January – a bitterly cold day – Winchester's enemy arrived.

Procter had learned three days before that Reynolds and his men had been pushed out of Frenchtown. Recognizing that the Americans were exposed, the lieutenant colonel set out from Upper Canada's Fort Amherstburg, at the mouth of the Detroit river. He took all available men – 597 in total – leaving the fort all but deserted. Accompanying Procter's force were more than 500 Native American warriors, including many who had been displaced by Harrison's brutality. The lieutenant colonel's assault on Winchester's troops at Frenchtown began poorly. The combined force of British, Canadians and Native Americans approached the village just before dawn. However, Procter chose to hold off the assault until his cannons were in place. Several minutes passed before an American guard spotted movement. His single shot, the first of the Battle of Frenchtown, killed a grenadier named

Gates. Procter's men opened fire on what they perceived as a line of troops, only to discover in the light of the breaking dawn that wooden pickets had been their targets. The artillery proved itself to be within American rifle range, resulting in needless casualties. Winchester's Kentucky sharpshooters proved to have great effect, until a charge by the Canadians and Native Americans broke his right flank. The Americans fled across the frozen river just as their general rode to join the battle. With Allen and Lewis, Winchester attempted to re-establish the right flank. However, they soon joined the hundreds of men running to the south of the Raisin, leaving the left flank to again fight on alone.

There was no security to be gained in their flight; indeed, the situation was much graver. After reaching the south shore, the Americans found themselves boxed in by Potawatomi warriors, whose people had been victimized by Harrison's search and destroy policy. More than 100 of Winchester's men were killed and then scalped. A final desperate rally in a snowy orchard some 2 km inland also met with failure.

A wounded Allen fought off an attempt at capture and was shot dead, while Winchester and Lewis surrendered to Roundhead, chief of the Wyandot. With the general's 17-year-old son, they were taken to Procter. The British commander had a certain upper hand. With Harrison's troops far away at the Maumee rapids, the Americans fighting from within the protection of the village had no chance of victory. Yet, when Procter suggested that it would be best for Winchester to surrender his men, the American general responded that his command had devolved upon the senior officers within the pickets of Frenchtown.

Borrowing a tactic used by the late Major General Sir Isaac Brock, Procter told Winchester that he could not be held responsible for the actions of the Native American warriors once his planned attack was in progress. The British and Canadian troops withdrew, awaiting the return of the warriors from the south shore of the Raisin. During the lull, Winchester reconsidered Procter's words and agreed to attempt surrender. Under a flag of truce, Procter met with Major George Madison, the American senior officer within Frenchtown. It was a tense negotiation. Fearing the Native American warriors, Madison would not capitulate until Procter agreed that the Americans would be protected from any attempt at retaliation. Many of Madison's men felt betrayed in the surrender; 33 of them escaped.

Winchester lost more than 400 men; more than 700 of his soldiers were taken prisoner. His great defeat was followed by Procter's disgrace. Though he had promised their protection, the next morning 64 wounded American prisoners were killed by Native American warriors.

Winchester's failure at Frenchtown ended not only his career but Harrison's drive towards Fort Detroit. The charismatic general withdrew up the Maumee, where he built Fort Meigs. Procter was aware of this new outpost, yet did nothing to prevent its construction. Neither this lapse, nor the murders of the wounded American soldiers had any effect on his military career; within months he was promoted to the ranks of brigadier general and major general.

THE BATTLE *of* YORK

27 APRIL 1813

——•——

DURING THE WINTER of 1813, the first of the war, both sides had focused a great amount of attention and resources on shipbuilding. The British looked to assure their dominance of Lake Erie through the construction of a new warship at Amherstburg. The United States Navy, meanwhile, sought to gain control by building an entire fleet at Presque Isle and Black Rock. Activity on Lake Ontario was just as busy. Frigates were being built at both Kingston and York, the two largest settlements in Upper Canada, while the Americans worked to complete a fleet at Sackets Harbor in New York State.

Of the two lakes, Ontario was considered to be of greater strategic value. The Americans had come to believe that naval superiority on this particular body of water could determine the entire war. A new strategy was adopted, in which the greatest prize was Kingston. If captured, it would sever the British supply line to Upper Canada. This most western colony of British North America would then fall, providing an opportunity to move down the Saint Lawrence river to the great Lower Canadian city of Montreal.

As the United States Navy raced to complete their ships and spring approached, American Major General Henry Dearborn, now commander of the Army of the Center at Sackets Harbor, Oswego and the Niagara river, began to question the new plan. He had become certain that 3,000 British regulars and as many as 5,000 other troops were guarding Kingston. Dearborn had no intelligence to support his conviction, and was challenged by Commodore Isaac Chauncey. However, both men agreed that the British were well aware of the new strategy and had made preparations for an assault on Kingston. Again, there was no intelligence to support this belief. In fact, the force at Kingston consisted of no more than 900 British regulars, supported by a very small number of local militiamen.

Ever cautious, Dearborn and Chauncey lowered their sights to a much smaller target: York. Though the capital of

Upper Canada, a position it had held for nearly two decades, York was little more than a small town. Its population of approximately 700 was protected by a small garrison containing the Government House Battery with two 12-lb (5-kg) guns, 1 km to the west. Another battery, the Western Battery, contained two obsolete 6-lb (2.5-kg) guns. Lacking guns, a third outpost, the Half-Moon Battery, might not be considered a battery at all.

Dearborn and Chauncey succeeded in converting John Armstrong, the American Secretary of War, to their proposed strategy. The new fleet having been completed, they had only to wait until Sackets Harbor was free of ice before carrying out their attack on York. This thaw was complete by 18 April, yet the major general and the commodore remained cautious; they allowed a further eight days to pass before setting sail.

On the evening of 26 April, Chauncey's squadron – a brig, a corvette and 12 schooners – approached the small colonial community. For several hours, they remained off the Scarborough Bluffs to the east of the town. On board the

14 ships were 1,800 men under the command of Dearborn and Brigadier General Zebulon Montgomery Pike.

The British and Canadian forces present at York – some 300 regulars and 300 militiamen – were severely outnumbered and outgunned. Defence of the capital fell to Major General Roger Hale Sheaffe, who, following the death of Sir Isaac Brock, had been made the Lieutenant Governor of Upper Canada.

The man who had driven back the Americans at the Battle of Queenston Heights, Sheaffe was a reluctant participant in the War of 1812. Decades earlier, the American Revolution had torn his family apart. Out of loyalty to the mother country, he had left his home in Boston, while his sister had chosen to remain.

Having spent the evening anchored off Scarborough Bluffs, the next morning the American fleet sailed past both York and its garrison. They landed at the ruins of Rouillé, an old fortification of New France.

Having watched as the American ships passed to the west, Sheaffe dispatched a group of approximately 100 Native

Americans to confront the invaders. This small group, under the command of Major James Givens, was meant to be supported by members of the Glengarry Light Infantry, but the company lost its way in the maze of paths through the woods outside the town. Though they eventually found their bearings and achieved the enemy's landing point, the American advance party had already landed. Several Glengarries were cut down as green-clad American riflemen made their way through the dense forest.

The Grenadier Company of the 8th Regiment of Foot met a similar fate. Trained for the open warfare of Europe, they fell victim to American sharpshooters who had taken cover behind logs and in the surrounding forests. Their cries – 'Show us our enemy! Show us our enemy!' – went unanswered. All but 30 of their 119 members were killed. Among the dead was their captain, Neal McNeale.

His way having been cleared, Pike ordered an advance on York's Western Battery. His men hauled two 6-pounder (2.5 kg) field guns through the woods, a feat Sheaffe had thought impossible. Within their cramped quarters, the

British and Canadians worked to revive the obsolete, broken cannons. Although Pike had not yet begun using his big guns, the battery had fallen under a heavy barrage from six of Chauncey's ships. Disaster soon stuck when, as the result of an accident, the battery's travelling magazine exploded. More than a dozen men were killed, while many others lay charred and maimed. Pike was able to seize the battery without resistance. The unarmed Half-Moon Battery fell with similar ease, thus opening an unopposed route to the garrison.

What Pike could not have known is that plans were at that moment being carried forth to abandon the garrison and its Government House Battery. Pummelled by the 24-pounder (11 kg) and 32-pounder (14 kg) cannons of Chauncey's schooner, the battery had proven itself ineffective. Sheaffe had decided to sacrifice the fort and, criminally, members of his militia. As the major general retreated towards York with his regulars, he left orders with senior militia officers to continue their fight with the Americans. Sheaffe's other order, which was unknown to these same militia officers, concerned the destruction of the garrison's magazine – cartridges, round shot and shells, with some 500 barrels of gunpowder.

Pike had ordered his men to halt, as the American cannons were being prepared. It is known that he expected to see a white flag being raised above the garrison. A British surrender would have been his greatest accomplishment; after more than ten months of fighting, he would be the first to accept a British surrender in the war.

It was not to be.

The explosion of the magazine sent an eruption of debris in all directions. Metal, stones, rocks, masonry and broken beams rained down on the Americans and the Canadian militiamen. Pike was found pinned by a gigantic boulder; a large hole had been torn in his back. As the brigadier general was carried away, barely alive, the surviving Canadian militia raised the much sought-after white flag above what remained of the garrison. Pike was transported to Chauncey's corvette, the USS *Madison*, where he died with his head resting on the captured Royal Standard. Pike was one of 200 who were either killed or maimed by the blast.

The detonation of the Government House Battery magazine was not the only act of destruction ordered by Sheaffe. With the knowledge that it would soon be in American hands, he made certain that the frigate nearing completion in the dockyard – HMS *Isaac Brock* – was set ablaze.

Although the lieutenant governor knew surrender to be inevitable, he would take no part. Instead, he continued to march his regulars eastwards, with the intention of reinforcing Kingston. The responsibility for negotiations leading to surrender devolved to Lieutenant Colonel William Chewett, the elderly surveyor general, and militia major William Allan, a merchant.

There was considerable resentment among the Americans owing to the fact that HMS *Isaac Brock* had been torched even though the flag of surrender had been raised. Moreover, Sheaffe and his regulars had continued on to Kingston, leaving negotiations to a couple of amateur soldiers.

Progress was slow, in part due to Major General Dearborn's refusal to leave the safety of the USS *Madison*.

As the negotiations crawled, the Reverend John Strachan, who had the previous year accepted the rectorship of York, took it upon himself to board the American corvette. Once there he accused the major general of intentionally delaying capitulation, thereby allowing American troops to reek havoc.

The strong-willed Strachan assumed the leadership role in negotiations. The Reverend lacked leverage, and eventually settled on an agreement which brought him no happiness. All arms and public stores were to be given up to the invaders; the militia would be paroled; all officers were to be imprisoned; private property would be respected.

However, the two American officers charged with carrying the terms of surrender for ratification did not return from behind their lines. In their stead, a third officer arrived and placed Allan under arrest. With the capitulation still not ratified, other militia officers soon followed the negotiator into American imprisonment.

That evening, mayhem of a different sort began. The House of Assembly was plundered; this included the office of the clerk, Donald McLean, who had been killed along with so many grenadiers only hours earlier. With Dearborn's knowledge, private homes were entered and looted. Those who dared complain to the major general were told that he could not offer protection.

The next morning, Strachan again confronted Dearborn, accusing him of delaying the signing of the terms of surrender so that his soldiers might plunder York. Under the barrage of the angered clergyman, the major general quickly reread and signed the document. Nearly 20 hours after the flag of surrender had been raised and all fighting had ceased, the Battle of York had officially come to an end. Sixty-two Britons and Canadians had been killed, with a further 94 wounded. The American figures, though less accurate, reflected even greater carnage: a total of 320 were reported either dead or wounded.

And yet, the plundering continued, with the Reverend Strachan's own church among the targets. Several other public buildings were looted and set on fire, including the lieutenant governor's house and the parliament buildings.

On 8 May, a miserable spring day, the Americans finally left York for Fort Niagara in New York State. Eleven days had passed since they had attacked and had succeeded in driving Sheaffe and his troops into retreat. It might be said that the lieutenant governor was still in retreat. His march overland to Kingston would take three more days. After his leadership or lack thereof was roundly criticized by the Provincial Assembly, he lost both his military and public offices in Upper Canada. He returned to the United Kingdom, where he eventually achieved the rank of general.

The town of York recovered from the destruction wrought by Dearborn's men. In the decade that followed, its population rose 12-fold. In 1834, the community was incorporated as a city. The name 'York', shared by several other settlements in Upper Canada, was replaced with 'Toronto', a Huron word meaning 'place of meeting'. Its first mayor was William Lyon Mackenzie, who three years later led the Rebellion of Upper Canada and instigated the Battle of Montgomery's Tavern.

Retaliation for the burning of York came in August 1814. After the defeat of the American militia at Bladensburg, Maryland, British troops marched into Washington, where they set the capital city's public buildings aflame. The Capital Building, the Treasury, the War Office, the dockyards and the offices of the *National Intelligencer*, the government's propaganda newspaper, were all burned. As President James Madison fled to Virginia, his wife, Dolley, watched the White House burn from the safety of a friend's home.

THE BATTLE *of* FORT GEORGE
25–27 MAY 1813

———◆———

THE BATTLE OF York had, at long last, given the Americans a victory of significance in the War of 1812. Although they abandoned their occupation, Commodore Isaac Chauncey and Major General Henry Dearborn had left the town defenceless. They took with them a great number of materials, including 20 24-pounder (11-kg) carronades, intended for the squadron under construction at Lake Erie. The brig HMS *Duke of Gloucester*, which had been in a poor state of repair at the dockyard, was also seized. While HMS *Isaac Brock*, torched under orders from Major General Roger Hale Sheaffe, was beyond salvage, it was one less warship with which the United States Navy would have to contend.

It was true that the original target, Kingston, remained untouched. Nevertheless the American campaign of 1813 had begun very well. Bolstered by success, the previously cautious Chauncey boldly declared: 'We may consider the upper province as conquered.'

From York, the victorious Americans sailed south across Lake Ontario. It was not an easy passage. The commodore was forced to ride out a severe spring storm. Illness set in, affecting Dearborn among others.

The original strategy intended that his force would make a swift amphibious assault at Fort George on the Canadian side of the mouth of the Niagara river. Instead, the 16 warships under Chauncey's command ended up transporting Dearborn's men to the American Fort Niagara on the river's opposing shore. There, it was believed, the major general and his men would restore health and energy before again engaging the British and Canadians. The plan was quickly exposed as ill considered. No provision had been made to accommodate the approximately 1,800 soldiers and sailors who had quite suddenly appeared at Fort Niagara. As a result, officers aside, all suffered through several days of food shortages.

Although Dearborn had claimed victory at the Battle of York, he had not set foot on shore until many hours after the last shots had been fired. True credit belonged to Zebulon Montgomery Pike, who had died not long after the flag of surrender had been raised. The deceased brigadier general's replacement was Colonel Winfield Scott. Placed in British custody after surrendering at the Battle of Queenston Heights, Scott had since been freed through a prisoner exchange. On 15 May, he took up his new role as Dearborn's chief of staff.

Confident where the brigadier general was cautious and inspired where the brigadier general was indecisive, Scott immediately improved the administration of Dearborn's Army of the Center. His drive was matched by that of naval Lieutenant Oliver Hazard Perry, who had accepted an appointment as one of Chauncey's senior officers.

Both men had considerable influence on the attack on Fort George. The new plan involved a force of 2,000 divided into four waves, all of which would land off Lake Ontario. Support would be provided by the corvette USS *Madison* and the USS *Oneida*, a brig, which would engage the nearby British batteries. Twelve schooners, each mounting a single heavy cannon, would hug the shore.

As he had at York, Dearborn would take in the action from the *Madison*. Major General Morgan Lewis, his second-in-command, would have nominal command of the landing force.

The assault on Fort George began not by land, but by air. On 25 May, the Americans began a bombardment from Fort Niagara and positions along the riverbank. The cannonballs sent hurling across the Niagara were 'hot shot'. Heated in furnaces, they were quickly loaded into cannons and fired. As a result many buildings that survived the impacts subsequently burned to the ground.

Command of Fort George, indeed all the British and Canadian forces on the Niagara peninsula, fell to Brigadier General John Vincent. Recognizing that an American invasion was imminent, but not knowing where it would take place, he had attempted to cover the threatened front. The majority of his 1,700 men – approximately 1,200 regulars and 500 militia – had taken up position along the shore of the Niagara, his assumption being that the assault would be covered by the cannons of the American fort.

Early on the morning of 27 May, after nearly two days of shelling, the enemy finally drew near. Their approach was covered by a thick fog. Vincent, who was standing near the Canadian lighthouse at the time, was met with the sight of 16 American warships spread out over a 2-mile arc, moving towards the Canadian shore. In tow were a further 134 craft – bateaux, scows and boats – carrying artillery and thousands of American invaders. As Vincent rode off to Fort George, the guns on the lake, numbering 51 in total, began to fire. The battery at the lighthouse was destroyed, while another at Two Mile Creek, 2 km to the west, was abandoned.

It was there that the first wave of Americans, under Scott, landed. They were met by a company of the Glengarry Light Infantry. After charging the enemy as it waded ashore the Glengarries were forced to retreat, leaving half their number as casualties. A company of the Royal

Newfoundland Fencibles followed, but were cut down by grapeshot fired by the American warships.

Scott's men, consisting of the United States 1st Rifle Regiment, two companies of the 15th Infantry and the bulk of the 2nd Artillery, advanced inland, where they were counter-attacked by what remained of the Glengarries and the Royal Newfoundland Fencibles, along with five companies of the 8th Regiment of Foot, and more than 100 militiamen. Scott was driven back, despite the heavy losses suffered by the British and Canadians from heavy fire on Lake Ontario. Any slim chance the British and Canadians had of turning back the invaders came to an end, however, when the second wave of Americans landed, thereby providing hundreds of reinforcements.

To the west, Vincent prepared to abandon Fort George. He knew that the battered fortification would soon be surrounded, leaving those inside at the mercy of cannonballs being fired from Fort Niagara and the American warships. Outside Fort George, the town of Newark – present-day Niagara-on-the-Lake – also came under fire, not only from the lake, but from the 20 heavy guns at Fort Niagara.

Vincent ordered that the artillery be spiked and the storage magazines be set alight. However, these tasks were performed in such haste that the Americans entered to find that nearly all damage to the fort had been caused not by Vincent's troops, but by themselves. The only one of the magazines to explode knocked Scott from his horse, breaking his collarbone. This injury, not nearly as serious as that which felled Pike under similar circumstances at the Battle of York, did not prevent Scott from beginning a pursuit of the retreating British and Canadians.

Vincent and his force were now retreating towards Queenston. This move southwards had been anticipated. On the American side of the Niagara, Colonel James Burn and his dragoons were to have crossed the river to intercept Vincent and his men. However, fire from British batteries had delayed the crossing, allowing the British and Canadians to pass beyond the planned point of attack. When he finally arrived on the Canadian shore, Burn worked with Scott to join forces in chasing their enemy. In the few minutes it took to reorganize, word reached Scott that Major General Morgan Lewis was ordering his men back to Fort George.

The commander of the third and final wave to land near Two Mile Creek – long after the fighting had stopped – Lewis was anything but a career soldier. As a former chief justice and governor of New York State, the brother-in-law of the Secretary of War and childhood friend of President James Madison, he had achieved his rank through political and personal connections. This influence found its way on to the battlefield in another way when Dearborn, watching all from aboard the USS *Madison*, decided to turn direct command over to Lewis.

The major general shared Dearborn's cautious nature; Fort George was now in American hands and he did not want to risk its loss. Scott, who had been convinced that he was only 70 minutes away from defeating Vincent and his men, was forced to return to the fort. The British and Canadian retreat continued, unchallenged.

In the Battle of Fort George the Americans achieved their second major victory of the war; it was also the first in which British and Canadian fatalities outstripped their own. Thirty-nine Americans were killed, thirteen fewer than those lost by the enemy.

THE BATTLE *of* BEAVER DAMS

24 JUNE 1813

———•———

IN THE MONTH that led to the Battle of Beaver Dams, the Americans had struggled to build upon their victory at Fort George. However, a decisive British and Canadian victory on 6 June in the Battle of Stoney Creek had shaken morale. What's more, the Americans found themselves weakened in force when the flotilla of warships supporting the army on the Niagara peninsula was reassigned to counter threats to their own base. The invading soldiers withdrew to Fort George, pursued by the British and Canadians who occupied outposts at Twelve Mile Creek and at Beaver Dams. From these two stations, militia and Mohawk warriors staged raids on American supply lines and communications.

It fell to Brigadier General John Parker Boyd to deal with the raiders and restore his men's confidence. This, he determined, could be accomplished through a surprise attack on the outpost at Beaver Dams. Boyd organized a force consisting of detachments of the 6th, 13th and 23rd United States Infantry, the whole of the 14th Infantry, a company of artillery with two 6-pounder (2.5-kg) field guns, 20 United States Dragoons and 40 mounted New York Militia volunteers. He selected as commander the 14th Infantry's Colonel Charles Boerstler.

On 23 June, as night fell on a rain-drenched day, Boerstler's force quietly and secretly left Fort George, marching toward the village of Queenston and the nearby hamlet of Saint David's. Their guide, a native of Buffalo named Cyrenius Chapin, proved to be a blundering incompetent who had little knowledge of the countryside. Arriving at Queenston just before midnight, they had managed to travel only 11 km in their first day. There they took quarters in outbuildings and houses, including one belonging to James Secord, a militia captain. Secord, they recognized, was of no threat. Eight months earlier, he had been injured gravely in the Battle of Queenston Heights, and had been lame ever since.

According to legend, his wife, Laura Secord, overheard American officers discussing the planned assault and decided to warn the soldiers at Beaver Dams. In the early hours of 23 June, she set out on what would be a 30-km trek. Although the Americans had placed sentries around the village, prohibiting anyone from leaving, Secord's story that she was going to milk a cow was believed. She made her way through the woods until she came across a Mohawk encampment. From there she was escorted to Lieutenant James FitzGibbon, who was commanding the Beaver Dams outpost. FitzGibbon then positioned 400 Mohawk warriors along the route intended by the Americans, in a thickly wooded area a little more than 2 km east of the outpost.

The force consisted of two groups: 300 warriors were nominally commanded by Captain Dominique Ducharme and a further 100 by Captain William Johnson Kerr. FitzGibbon was in reserve with no more than 46 men of the 49th Regiment of Foot.

The next morning, Boerstler and his men departed from Queenston as planned. As his force approached the outpost at Beaver Dams, the colonel became aware of the Mohawks closing in through the woods; yet he held fast to his plan. The warriors opened fire. Among the first casualties was Boerstler himself. Wounded, but not severely, he was placed in a wagon. The Americans were powerless as the Mohawks continued sniping. Though they returned fire, Boerstler's men seemed unable to hit anything through the cover of dense forest. Demoralized and fearful of a massacre, it was a relief when FitzGibbon approached under a flag of truce. The Canadian lieutenant told the wounded Boerstler that his force was vastly outnumbered. It was a bold lie; in fact, though only slightly, the Americans had the greater number. FitzGibbon then added that barring an American surrender, he could not guarantee the actions of the Mohawk warriors; it was entirely possible that all would perish. At this, the American commander capitulated, surrendering his force of 484 men.

Shortly after, when describing the battle, FitzGibbon wrote:

Not a shot was fired on our side by any but the Natives.
They beat the American detachment into a state of

terror, and the only share I claim is taking advantage of a favorable moment to offer them protection from the tomahawk and scalping knife.

The brief Battle of Beaver Dams took the lives of five Mohawk warriors and 56 Americans. While it was later claimed by the Americans that a number of their wounded were scalped by the Mohawks, no evidence of this was ever produced.

Dearborn learned the details of the surrender at Beaver Dams by way of a letter penned by Boerstler himself. After signing 'Your distressed humble servant', the lieutenant colonel added: 'I presume my destination will be Quebec, I beg that I may be exchanged as soon as possible.'

In Washington, news of the defeat was followed by demands for Dearborn's removal. The mood was perhaps best reflected in the words of Congressman Charles Ingersoll, who described the event as the 'climax of continual mismanagement and misfortune'. Dearborn would soon find himself removed from the war.

Within the walls of Fort George, the opportunity for a

boost in confidence had all but vanished. Morale was driven lower still when, two weeks later, 28 men were killed while attempting to pursue an enemy detachment led by Mohawk chief John Norton.

While the Americans continued to occupy Fort George, patrols beyond the vicinity of its walls all but came to an end. In September, Boyd and the vast majority of regulars were reassigned to Sackets Harbor. On 10 December, as winter fell, the remaining Americans abandoned the fort that had cost so many lives the previous May.

Although it was one of the smaller battles of the War of 1812, the Battle of Beaver Dams is one of the better known. This is due entirely to the involvement of Laura Secord. Frequently characterized as the greatest Canadian heroine, her origins are often ignored. She was, in fact, a loyalist immigrant who was born in Massachusetts in the year leading up to the American Revolution.

Her story of heroism, which has been questioned by some historians, is supported by FitzGibbon's own contradictory testimonials.

In one such testimonial, dated 1827, FitzGibbon wrote:

I do hereby Certify that on the 22d. day of June 1813, Mrs. Secord, Wife of James Secord, Esqr. then of St. David's, came to me at the Beaver Dam after Sun Set, having come from her house at St. David's by a circuitous route a distance of twelve miles, and informed me that her Husband had learnt from an American officer the preceding night that a Detachment from the American Army then in Fort George would be sent out on the following morning (the 23d.) for the purpose of Surprising and capturing a Detachment of the 49th Regt. then at Beaver Dam under my Command. In Consequence of this information, I placed the Natives under Norton together with my own Detachment in a Situation to intercept the American Detachment and we occupied it during the night of the 22d. – but the Enemy did not come until the morning of the 24th when his Detachment was captured. Colonel Boerstler, their commander, in a conversation with me confirmed fully the information communicated to me by

Mrs. Secord and accounted for the attempt not having been made on the 23rd. as at first intended.

In this account, Secord learned of the American plans and made her exit from Saint David's the day before Boerstler and his men set out from Fort George.

It is probable that Mohawk scouts had already warned FitzGibbon of the approaching Americans.

THE BATTLE *of* THE THAMES
5 OCTOBER 1813

THE WORST CANADIAN defeat in the war, the Battle of the Thames was the direct result of an earlier conflict, the Battle of Lake Erie, which had been fought off the coast of Ohio. Fought between the Royal Navy and the United States Navy, the outcome had dire consequences for Upper Canada.

On 10 September, a British squadron of six ships – a corvette, a schooner, two sloops and two brigs – confronted five schooners, a sloop and three brigs of the United States Navy. It was an uneven match. The British disadvantage was created, in part, by the capture of the ordnance and supplies destined for Lake Erie at the Battle of York. In a battle that lasted just under three hours, the Americans achieved a victory without precedent: a full British fleet had been defeated and captured whole by its enemy. As a result, the Royal Navy lost the lake they had controlled since the earliest days of the war.

The British defeat placed the territory they had captured in 1812 in jeopardy. With no naval presence, they would be unable to prevent the Americans from landing wherever and whenever they wished. Fearing the loss of his supply lines, Major General Henry Procter, the commander of the British and Canadian forces on the western front, decided to abandon Forts Detroit and Amherstburg. The latter was in a particularly vulnerable position as its cannon had been used to arm the corvette HMS *Detroit*, which had been captured by the Americans during the Battle of Lake Erie. Facing an inevitable invasion, Procter decided to retreat to a defensive position in the Thames river valley.

It was a strategy that Tecumseh could not abide. The great Shawnee leader argued that the British, Canadians and Native Americans should rise to confront any invasion, but Procter was deaf to his inspired speech. Perceiving cowardice in Procter, Tecumseh requested that the major general arm his warriors so that they might be able to stay behind and fight. 'Our lives are in the hands of the Great Spirit', he told Procter. 'We are determined to defend our land; and if it is his will, we wish to leave our bones upon it.' Again, he was ignored.

Tecumseh despised the major general for retreating, likening him to 'a fat animal that carries its tail upon its back. But when affrightened, it drops it between his legs and runs off'. To the leader of the Native American confederacy, Procter had none of the strength, bravery or intelligence of his departed friend Sir Isaac Brock.

Procter's retreat was slow, taking 12 days in total, a pace which might be explained by a belief that the American fleet had been so damaged in the Battle of Lake Erie that it would not be able to respond speedily. It was a disorderly withdrawal, marred by defections and a lack of provisions. All the way, British and Canadian troops were covered by Native American warriors.

The retreating troops were trailed by Major General William Henry Harrison. Tecumseh's old enemy first took Fort Amherstburg, which the Americans were surprised to find abandoned. From there Harrison and more than 3,500 men – both infantry and cavalry – followed Procter for the length of the Detroit river, along the southern shore of Lake Saint Clair, and nearly 60 km up the valley of the Thames river. Their progress was made easy by Procter's failure to destroy bridges.

Tecumseh pleaded several times with the major general to halt and face the pursuing army, but Procter held to the idea of making their stand at the village of Chatham. Upon arrival, the Native American leader was incensed to discover that Procter had not built the fortification he promised. The major general and his men had progressed some 30 km beyond the intended battlefield to the western side of Moraviantown, a peaceful community of Christian Munsee Native Americans.

It was here that, at long last, Procter confronted Harrison. The decision was not one of his choosing. The British and Canadians were down to half rations, a situation that could only worsen as Harrison had captured their supply boats. Procter's force had been reduced in number owing to stragglers who had been captured by the pursuing Americans. By the time he chose to turn and fight, Procter had little more than 600 soldiers, supported by 500 of Tecumseh's warriors.

In preparation, Procter formed his regulars in line of battle, planning to trap the Americans on the banks of the Thames. Meanwhile, the warriors took up positions in a swamp on the regulars' right in order to flank the enemy.

Harrison, who recognized his opponent's strategy, appeared indecisive. The two forces remained motionless while the American major general convened a council of war. It was determined that their best chance lay in a bayonet charge against the British left flank. Brigadier General George Trotter, whom Harrison chose to lead the attack, was a logical choice; a great many of his men knew those who had been victims of the massacre that had taken place at the River Raisin after the Battle of Frenchtown.

After an hour spent moving his men into position, Harrison received news of a flaw in his plan of attack: Trotter's men would be forced to traverse a swamp. An alternate plan was proposed, one in which mounted volunteers would ride through the swamp to attack the British left flank.

To the cry of 'Remember the Raisin!' the Americans charged. The British cannons failed and the Americans broke through despite the warriors' flanking fire. The British regulars turned and fled from the field. Unable to stop his men, Procter joined their retreat. He rode quickly, all too aware that the pursuing Kentuckians held him directly responsible for the Frenchtown massacre.

Tecumseh and his 500 warriors were now outnumbered by a factor of seven to one. The Shawnee chief urged his warriors on until his voice was forever silenced by an American musket ball which entered near his heart. The fighting ended as news of his death spread among his men.

Thirty-three of those killed on the British side were Native American warriors, a reflection of their determination. Twelve Britons and Canadians were killed, 35 wounded and 442 others surrendered and were taken prisoner. The American casualties, nearly all at the hands of Tecumseh's warriors, amounted to 15 killed and 30 wounded.

It was in keeping with Harrison's history that his next move was to send his troops on to Moraviantown. Although the community had had no involvement in the conflict, the major general ordered that the settlement be burned to the ground.

A decisive victory for the Americans, the Battle of the Thames gave them near complete control over the north-west frontier. However, Upper Canada was spared more bloodshed. Harrison, recognizing that his supplies were growing thin and that winter was approaching, withdrew to Fort Detroit. After the burning of Moraviantown, he never moved to exploit his success. Whereas 14 months earlier the north-west front had served as the stage for the first assault on Canada, it remained quiet for the remainder of the war.

While the British and Canadians had lost a heroic ally in the death of Tecumseh, the Native Americans had lost their greatest leader. Without his guidance, the confederacy he had worked so hard to build effectively vanished.

News of Tecumseh's death was cause for celebration in

Washington; a formidable opponent in expansionist plans had been eliminated. Recognizing the political advantage to be gained, many men claimed to have been the Shawnee chief's killer. The most prominent of these was Colonel Richard Mentor Johnson, who had led the first charge against the British and Canadians, and who used the situation to gain the office the vice-president of the United States.

Major General Henry Procter's future was not quite so bright. A little more than a year after the Battle of the Thames, as 1814 drew to a close, he was tried by court martial for his conduct during the retreat. He was found guilty of 'deficiency in energy and judgement', and suspended for six months without pay. Although the conviction was later reduced to a reprimand, the verdict ended his military career. Procter returned to his native England in 1815, and died seven years later.

Major General William Henry Harrison resigned from the military before the war ended, a decision which would be used by his opponents in his 1840 bid for the White

House. He countered with a campaign drawing on his reputation as a hero in the wars against Tecumseh and the Native American confederacy. Its slogan, 'Tippecanoe and Tyler, Too' – referring to the Battle of Tippecanoe and John Tyler, his running-mate – remains one of the most effective in American political history.

Harrison enjoyed an easy victory. On 4 March 1841, he was sworn in as the ninth President of the United States. His time in office was short. Thirty days later, Harrison was dead from pneumonia. His death was the first in a series of seven which claimed every president elected in a year ending with a zero. The next six eligible men – Abraham Lincoln, James Garfield, William McKinley, Franklin Delano Roosevelt and John F. Kennedy – all died in office. American folklore has dubbed this string of tragedy the 'Curse of Tecumseh'.

THE BATTLE *of* THE CHÂTEAUGUAY
26 OCTOBER 1813

———•———

THE CAPTURE OF Montreal had long been an objective of the War Hawks and those running the war in the Madison administration. The most rapidly growing city in the Canadas, its population was approaching 20,000 and would soon surpass that of Quebec City. Unlike its rival, it was thought to be an easier target. Montreal had none of the natural fortification that Quebec had exploited to great effect throughout its history.

The seizure of Montreal, so the Americans thought, would sever the supply line along the Saint Lawrence river, bringing about the fall of Upper Canada. As this anticipated result was identical to that expected from a capture of Kingston, a battle raged within the American forces as to which city should be targeted first. An attack on Kingston had been a key part of the strategy drawn up the previous winter; indeed, it was to have been the starting point of the 1813 campaign. However, the hesitation, caution and unsubstantiated beliefs held by Commodore Isaac Chauncey and Major General Henry Dearborn had led to the rejection of the plan.

In July, shortly after the first anniversary of the start of the war, Dearborn had been recalled and reassigned to an administrative post in New York City. His replacement, Major General James Wilkinson, was the most peculiar of choices. A career soldier, his history was one marred by scandal, intrigue, trickery and incompetence. He had three times been obliged to resign his commissions, the first time owing to his involvement in the Conway Cabal, a conspiracy which had been designed to replace George Washington, then commander-in-chief of the Continental Army. Wilkinson's thorny past was well known, though he had managed to keep secret the oath of allegiance he had sworn to the Spanish crown.

Wilkinson had been appointed Dearborn's successor as

commander of the Army of the Center by his friend John Armstrong, the Secretary of War. The relationship between the two men was a shaky one. Two decades earlier, Wilkinson had accused Armstrong of fraud, a charge which disrupted their friendship and had led the future Secretary of War to resign from the army.

Working together again, the two men resumed their combative relationship. Still focused on the fall of Upper Canada, in August Armstrong wrote to his new commander to say that Kingston represented the '*first* and *great* object of the campaign'. Armstrong's response was that Montreal should be the target. Later the same month, the two men traded their positions. As Chauncey and Dearborn had before them, Wilkinson and Armstrong hesitated, not at all confident of success.

Meanwhile, 4,000 regulars and 1,500 militia awaited orders at Châteauguay Four Corners, just south of the border between Lower Canada and New York State. Armstrong wrote to their commander, Major General Wade Hampton, that his troops must hold fast 'to keep up the enemy's doubts, with regard to the real point of your attack'. This letter, written near the end of September, was premature – there still had been no decision as to which city would be on the receiving end of the American assault.

A wealthy southern plantation owner, Hampton had been orphaned in a Cherokee raid as a youth. He had worked hard to achieve his success, including that as a military man. Hampton and his men had been waiting at Châteauguay Four Corners since 25 September. As the weeks passed with no instructions, Hampton began to fear that he and his men would have to winter at Châteauguay Four Corners. Finally, on 16 October, the major general received word from Armstrong that he was to move his men down the Châteauguay river and cross the border onto Canadian soil. And yet, even as Hampton's men set out, marching through an early snow, their destination remained undetermined.

As Hampton prepared his men to leave Châteauguay Four Corners, he was met with a significant setback; nearly all of the New York militia refused to leave their state, as was their right.

The Canadians were well aware of the American forces at Châteauguay Four Corners. Major General Louis de Watteville, the recently appointed commander of the Montreal District, had already ordered units of militia to be called up. The commander of the outposts, Lieutenant Colonel Charles-Michel d'Irumberry de Salaberry, had for months been receiving accurate intelligence from the farmers in the area.

On the north side of the Châteauguay, Salaberry ordered his corps, the Canadian Voltigeurs, several units of the Select Embodied Militia and local militia units to the Châteauguay river. On 22 October, he instructed the creation of breastworks. Two companies of Canadian Voltigeurs, one company of Canadian Fencibles, a militia company from Beauharnois and roughly 20 Mohawk warriors lay in wait behind the fallen trees. At a ford in the river, a little more than 1 km to the north of this force, Lieutenant Colonel George Macdonnell commanded a further three companies of Voltigeurs, another company of the Select Embodied Militia and approximately 150 Mohawk warriors. The varied force amounted to roughly 470 – outnumbered by a factor of more than eight to one.

Hampton knew of the Canadians on the north side of the Châteauguay river, and was aware of the ford. He chose Colonel Robert Purdy to lead more than 1,000 men along the south side. Following his strategy, the force would pass by the Canadians, then cross the ford to the north shore, thereby enabling them to outflank the enemy. A more direct assault would be made on the north side, from which Brigadier General George Izard would lead another force of more than 1,000 men.

After Hampton had dispatched Purdy, he received orders from Armstrong to construct winter quarters for 10,000 men on the Saint Lawrence river. There would, he realized, be no attack on Montreal. It was, however, too late to call Purdy back to camp. The colonel and his men marched through the swamp and underbrush, led by ineffective guides who had warned them that they had no real knowledge of the terrain.

On 26 October, as the sun rose, Purdy came under fire

from the Canadians who had been dispatched to guard the ford. If only to escape enemy fire, the Americans moved further north, where they were confronted by Macdonell and his men.

On the north side of the Châteauguay, Izard realized that the battle had begun. He moved to confront the Canadians who were protected by the breastworks. When one of the invaders stepped forward crying, 'Brave Canadians, surrender yourselves; we wish you no harm!' Salaberry himself shot the American dead.

As Izard's troops moved forward in a fashion more suited to the open warfare of a European theatre, they were met with the return fire of individual gunmen. The Mohawk war cries combined with the cheers and bugle calls of the Canadians to unnerve the Americans. Thinking that they were outnumbered, they retreated.

Two Canadians and 23 Americans were killed in the battle; the number of wounded – 15 Canadians to 33 Americans – was slightly more balanced. A further 29 Americans were reported missing, presumably having deserted.

Hampton returned to Châteauguay Four Corners, where he held a council of war. All involved concluded that any renewed advance would only be met with failure. From their base, the force moved further south to the more hospitable town of Plattsburgh.

For Salaberry, 26 October was 'a glorious day'. His force of 470 men – Canadians all – had repulsed 4,000 American invaders. On the evening that followed the battle, Salaberry wrote to his father: 'I have won a victory mounted on a wooden horse.'

THE BATTLE *of* CRYSLER'S FARM

11–12 NOVEMBER 1813

ON 28 OCTOBER, Major General James Wilkinson, the commander of the Army of the Center, wrote to John Armstrong, the United States Secretary of War, 'All our hopes have been very nearly blasted.' Wilkinson knew nothing of the American defeat at the Battle of the Châteauguay two days earlier; he was referring to inclement weather and sickness, much of it the result of food poisoning, that had weakened his troops.

Suffering from dysentery, Wilkinson continued to display the indecision that was so much a part of his character. It was not until 30 October that he announced his intention to launch an attack on Montreal. Commodore Isaac Chauncey was, in his own words, 'mortified' by the decision. Kingston, the alternate target, was little more than 30 km to the north-west, while Montreal lay hundreds of kilometres to the east. With winter approaching, Chauncey felt that Wilkinson's objective had precious little chance of success. Mortification was joined by resentment, as he felt that his navy had been reduced to a glorified transportation service.

Another week elapsed before the 8-km-long flotilla bound for Montreal – 6,000 men in more than 350 boats – finally launched.

As if to belie the commodore's arguments about the weather, the early days were blessed by an Indian summer. And yet, despite this good fortune, Wilkinson's progress was slow; he was behind schedule from the start.

On 6 November, the American flotilla landed at Morristown, New York. Just 16 km down the river lay Prescott, a small Canadian town with a stockade and cannons. In order to pass by the heavy guns, Wilkinson decided it best to remove all armaments and supplies from his boats for transportation by land; his troops would march along the shore while the lightly manned craft sailed past in the dark.

It was only then, when preparing the operation, that Wilkinson received word from Major General Wade Hampton of the American loss at the Châteauguay river. If there was any good news in the defeat, it lay in the fact that the vanquished force remained intact. Wilkinson sent word back to Hampton that they would now rendezvous at Saint Regis, across the Saint Lawrence from the Canadian town of Cornwall.

Under cover of night and fog, Wilkinson's boats successfully bypassed Prescott. However, the following day his flotilla came under fire from snipers and cannons, forcing Wilkinson to dispatch a corps of 1,200 men with orders to clear the Canadian shore. As the sun descended, the flotilla had progressed little more than 11 km.

Still suffering from dysentery, Wilkinson was consuming heavy doses of laudanum and whiskey. His natural pessimism began to prey upon his already limited confidence. Wilkinson had been told that his force was being pursued by two armed schooners and seven gunboats. What's more, interrogations of threatened Canadian farmers had yielded fantastic tales of formidable batteries, bloodthirsty savages and an approaching army consisting of more than 5,000 regulars and more than 20,000 militiamen.

On 9 November, Wilkinson had reinforcements sent to aid the corps clearing the riverbank. The flotilla was about to enter the Long Sault Rapids – 11 km in length. Meanwhile, the British gunboats had appeared and started to attack the rear.

The new threat came from a 'corps of observation' commanded by Lieutenant Colonel Joseph Wanton Morrison, which had been dispatched from Kingston. On 8 November, they managed to evade the ships of Chauncey's Lake Ontario fleet and had entered the Saint Lawrence. In less than two days, they had travelled the same distance that Wilkinson's flotilla had taken two weeks to cover. The accomplishment was made even greater by a stop at Prescott, where they received reinforcements, increasing their number from 650 to more than 1,400.

On the evening of 10 November, Morrison's force encamped adjacent to the farm of John Crysler, 2 km upriver from Wilkinson's flotilla.

The next morning, the gunboats resumed their fire on the American flotilla. Wilkinson was forced to recognize that the British would need to be driven away before the Long Sault could be approached. As the major general was still sick, the task fell to John Parker Boyd, the brigadier general who had ordered the ill-fated raid at Beaver Dams, and the 8,000 men placed under his command.

In setting up camp near Crysler's Farm, Morrison had hoped to draw the Americans to its large open fields. He favoured open battlegrounds typical of European warfare for which two of his regiments – the 49th and the 89th Regiment of Foot – had been trained. Knowing that his force was seriously outnumbered, the lieutenant colonel saw certain advantage in his highly disciplined British regulars. Wilkinson's fighters, on the other hand, were veterans of the Native American wars, bloody skirmishes in which individual action was key.

The Americans did not begin their assault until the afternoon, when Colonel Eleazer Wheelock Ripley and his 21st United States Infantry, intending to attack the British and Canadians from the rear, attempted to advance through the woods to the north of the open fields. They achieved some success at first, driving back a Canadian Voltigeur skirmish line, and forcing them into the field. The Americans chose to chase, making a fatal error. They emerged within the sights of the 89th, which formed the British and Canadian left flank. A fixed and unyielding line of regulars wheeled to face the scattered 21st Infantry, and fired in unison. While some Americans fled, others took cover in the woods, from which they made a futile attempt to engage the British.

Having failed on the left, Boyd ordered three brigades on his opponent's right flank to advance. His force fell victim immediately to the drill-like precision of the British regulars, and their assaults became increasingly disorderly. The British had encouraged some confusion by disguising members of the 49th, Sir Isaac Brock's old regiment, in the grey coats of militiamen. This deception proved particularly effective against the advancing 3rd Brigade.

Their commander, Brigadier General Leonard Covington attempted to buoy his men by calling out, 'Come, lads, let me see how you will deal with these militia men!' Moments later he struck the ground, mortally wounded. As Covington's second-in-command took the leadership, he was killed. After two more senior officers were lost, the brigade began a retreat.

As other Americans had also begun to withdraw, their artillery, hauled from the flotilla, began to arrive. Through a hail of grapeshot, the 49th moved in to capture the guns, while fighting off American dragoons sent to attempt an attack on the British rear. Their failure led to a general retreat.

In the end, the only real value brought by the American dragoons was in slowing the advance of the 49th, thus allowing the Americans to prevent the capture of all but one of their heavy guns.

Under a gathering autumn storm, the Americans withdrew to their boats and crossed the Saint Lawrence into New York State. Wilkinson encouraged Boyd to maintain a presence on the Canadian shore, if only to save face, but the brigadier general refused.

Reporting on the battle to Armstrong, his old nemesis and friend, Wilkinson resorted to distortion and lies. He wrote to the Secretary of War: 'The enemy were superior to us in numbers [*sic*], and greatly superior in position, and supported by 7 or 8 gunboats'. The strength of the British and Canadians he recorded as 2,170 and claimed that 500 of this number had become casualties. In fact, British and Canadian casualties amounted to 31 dead and 148 wounded. The Americans suffered even greater losses with 102 killed and 237 wounded. A further 106 wounded American soldiers were taken prisoner by the British.

The harsh reality did not prevent Wilkinson from declaring boldly to the Secretary of War, 'although the imperious obligations of duty did not allow me sufficient time to rout the enemy, they were beaten'.

Although the enemy had not been beaten, Morrison recognized that he could not prevent Wilkinson from continuing his passage down the Saint Lawrence. The next day, smaller in number, its supplies depleted, the flotilla managed to navigate the rapids at Long Sault.

More than 100 km west of Montreal, on 13 November Wilkinson abandoned his assault on the city. He used as his pretext a letter received from Hampton the previous day. With the roads impassable, supplies running low, his troops sick and dispirited, the major general had written that a rendezvous at Saint Regis was not possible. Hampton informed Wilkinson that he was instead leading his troops to Plattsburg from where he would pursue an invasion route involving Lake Champlain and the Richelieu river, similar to that used in 1775 by General Richard Montgomery. It is likely that the major general intended no such thing, and had already concluded that no invasion would be taking place.

Wilkinson made the audacious claim that with Hampton's men he would have seized Montreal within ten days. In a letter to Armstrong he said that the failure of the expedition lay entirely with the major general's 'outrage of every principle of subordination and discipline'.

Wilkinson's army attempted winter quarters at the

American hamlet of French Mills, on the Salmon river, but were eventually forced to withdraw due to a lack of food and clothing. As they relocated to Plattsburg, their major general was convalescing at his Malone, New York home. Although he had declared that the capture of Montreal had merely been postponed, Wilkinson made no further plans.

Back in Washington, Wilkinson's competency was questioned, yet he retained command of the Army of the Center. In mid-March of 1814, the major general led a force of more than 4,000 north from Lake Champlain into Lower Canada. After several days of marching they encountered a stone mill on the Lacolle river in which 180 regulars, militia and Royal Marines had taken refuge. Wilkinson laid siege, but once again succumbed to his absence of courage. Just as the British and Canadians were running out of ammunition, the American major general retreated until he was back on American soil. He set out for Washington, intending to be tried in a court of inquiry that he himself had requested. Wilkinson insisted that he be judged by a court composed of senior generals; however, as all fitting this description were engaged in the war, no trial could take place. His name was subsequently added to the unassigned list. Wilkinson would never again hold command.

In 1958, the site of the Battle of Crysler's Farm was submerged during the construction of the Saint Lawrence Seaway, a joint project of the Canadian and American governments.

THE BATTLE *of* LUNDY'S LANE
25 JULY 1814

———•—•———

THE BATTLE OF Lundy's Lane remains one of the most horrific and bloodiest struggles ever to take place on Canadian soil. It was fought on what might otherwise be described as a beautiful summer evening. Niagara Falls, the future honeymoon destination for millions of couples, roared just beyond sight of the battlefield.

The clash at Lundy's Lane was preceded by yet another American incursion – the third – into the Niagara peninsula. Not long after midnight on 3 July, a force of more than 1,000 men under the command of Major General Jacob Brown had crossed the Niagara river, not far from its source on Lake Erie. Fort Erie, the closest British position, was captured with ease.

Brown had been opposed to the war, and yet proved an aggressive, bold and adventurous adversary. His plan was next to capture the strategically important King's Bridge which spanned the Chippawa river to the north, then continue on to Fort George. There, with the expected support of a flotilla under Commodore Isaac Chauncey, Brown anticipated another victory. The fort, which the Americans had captured and then lost the previous year, would be his. Through the defeat of the British and Canadians at Fort George, he would achieve his ultimate goal – American control of the Niagara frontier, from Lake Erie to Lake Ontario.

This strategy was opposed by Brigadier General Eleazer Wheelock Ripley, a veteran of the Battle of Crysler's Farm, who thought it too risky for such a small force of men. Such was his conviction that Ripley tendered his resignation. Although Brown refused to accept it, he forever after considered the brigadier general to be an unreliable officer.

The next day, America's Independence Day, a brigade serving under Scott, who was Brown's other, more supportive brigadier general, reached the King's Bridge. On the north side of the Chippawa river, aware of the American advance, the British and Canadians dug in, preparing for the battle.

Confidence among those defending Upper Canada was high, and yet the clash that followed on 5 July – the Battle of Chippawa – was a clear and swift American victory. The British and Canadians were forced to flee and, within a few days, had fallen back to Fort George.

It might be said that the Americans had accomplished too much, too soon. As Ripley had argued, Brown hadn't nearly the force necessary to take the fort. Not only did he lack heavy artillery, it appeared than none was forthcoming. The American flotilla to which Brown had looked for support did not yet exist; Commodore Chauncey was still awaiting the completion of his new ships of war. In the meantime, the Royal Navy sailed, unchallenged in its control of Lake Ontario.

For nearly two weeks, the American force remained in occupation of Queenston, a few kilometres to the south of Fort George. Their commander, Brown, kept his watch on Lake Ontario 11 km to the north, convinced that he would soon see the white sails of Chauncey's squadron.

They never materialized.

As Brown kept his force in place, waiting for a non-existent flotilla, the British freely moved reinforcements and supplies to the fort from across the lake.

Pressure on Brown increased as the British, Canadians and Native Americans began to prey on the invaders' supply line. In the campaign's second week, he learned that a British contingent was on the move to the west of his position. The bad news provoked action. On 20 July, Brown ordered his men to Fort George. Lacking heavy artillery, there could be no assault; rather he attempted to lure the garrison out from behind the fortification. Brown wasted two days in this futile taunting, before returning with his men to Queenston. Once there the Americans set out even further south to the Chippawa river. The territory having been cast off, a British force under Major General Phineas Riall quickly marched his troops from Burlington to Lundy's Lane. Located roughly 6 km to the north of Brown's new position, the lane branched off from the main portage road on the Canadian shore of the Niagara river. As it ran along the summit of gently rising ground, the thoroughfare offered excellent views of the surrounding area. In repositioning his men, Riall recognized the distinct military advantage offered by the lane.

With no knowledge of Riall's new position, Brown worked to secure the American supply line at Chippawa. All was in preparation for an assault on Burlington, the location, he believed, of Riall's force.

Meanwhile, Lieutenant General Sir Gordon Drummond, the Lieutenant Governor of Upper Canada, was on Lake Ontario, travelling from York. He arrived at Fort George early on the morning of 25 July, ready to take command on the Niagara peninsula.

While Brown was unaware of Drummond's entrance that day, he received a sign that his assumption that placed Riall in Burlington was incorrect. Brown was informed by one of his officers that two companies of British infantry and a troop of dragoons were present at Wilson's Tavern, just a few kilometres north of his position. Though the major general did not believe the information to be accurate, he ordered Scott and a force of more than 1,200 men to the drinking establishment. Their approach was witnessed, through the aid of spyglasses, by a handful of British officers. One by one they departed on horseback as the Americans drew closer. The final officer waited until Scott's men were within musket range, whereupon he waved a military salute and rode away.

When the brigadier general finally reached the tavern, he was told by the proprietor, the widow Deborah Wilson, that Riall had indeed been present, along with 800 regulars and 300 militiamen. The numbers were incorrect – perhaps intentionally so. The enthusiastic Scott next made a fatal error in making no attempt to confirm Wilson's numbers. Instead, he sent word back to Brown at Chippawa that he was preparing to engage the enemy at Lundy's Lane.

Riall, too, had completely misjudged the strength of Scott's men. Having been informed by Native American scouts of American movement, he assumed, quite incorrectly, that the advancing troops represented Brown's entire army. Riall was convinced that his men were severely outnumbered, and so ordered them back to Queenston. However, as the

ABOVE: *An 1848 etching by Father Émile Rouargue depicting Major General William Phips attacking Quebec in 1690.*

LEFT: *Louis XV, the last French monarch to rule over Canadian territory.*

ABOVE: The Death of General Wolfe, *an 1857 painting by Alonzo Chappel.*

LEFT: The meeting of Isaac Brock
and Tecumseh, *as imagined in a
watercolour by C.W. Jeffreys.*

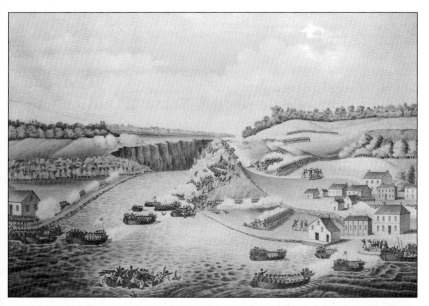

ABOVE: The Battle of Queenston. 18 October 1813, *an 1836 depiction of what has come to be known as the Battle of Queenston Heights. Note that the engagement actually took place on 13 October 1812.*

RIGHT: *General William Henry Harrison, commander of the Army of the Northwest during the War of 1812 and future President of the United States.*

ABOVE: *Tecumseh's death at the hand of Colonel Richard Mentor Johnson of Kentucky at the Battle of the Thames in 1813. According to Johnson, Tecumseh attacked with a tomahawk and was killed by a single pistol shot. Two decades later he led a successful campaign to become vice-president, using the slogan 'Rumpsey Dumpsey, Colonel Johnson killed Tecumseh'.*

BELOW: *A July 1882 portrait photograph of John Smoke Johnson, John Tutela and Young Warner, the last surviving Six Nations veterans of the War of 1812.*

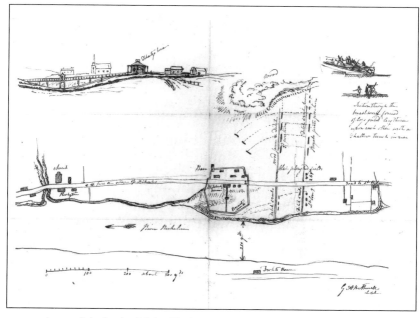

ABOVE: *A map of the Battle of Saint-Charles drawn by Lieutenant Colonel Wetherall on the day of his victory, 25 November 1837.*

BELOW: *The Battle of the Windmill, 1838, as seen from the American shore at Ogdensburg, New York.*

ABOVE: *Officers of the 60th Missiquoi Battalion at Eccles Hill, site of one of two Fenian raids on 25 May 1870.*

LEFT: *Louis Riel, the leader of both the Red River and North-West rebellions, perhaps the most controversial figure in Canadian history.*

New names in
Canadian history.

More are coming –
Will you be there?

ENLIST!

ABOVE: *Personnel of Royal Canadian Navy Beach Commando 'W' landing on Mike Beach, Juno sector of the Normandy beachhead during the D-Day Landings on 6 June 1944.*

BELOW: *The plan of the Normandy landings – forever known as D-Day.*

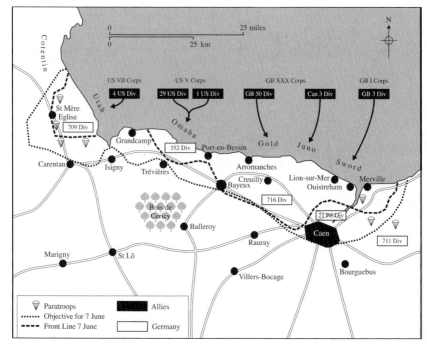

troops made their trek northwards, they encountered a column commanded by Drummond marching towards Lundy's Lane. The lieutenant governor countermanded Riall's order.

The British and Canadians began the process of reoccupying their position, placing their artillery – two 6-pounder (2.5-kg) and two 24-pounder (11-kg) guns, and one 5.5-inch (14-cm) howitzer – in a cemetery next to a small church which stood at the highest point of the ridge.

It was as he moved his troops into position that Scott realized the British and Canadian force was many times greater than the widow Wilson had led him to believe. While he considered withdrawing, Scott feared the effect such a retreat would have on both his own men and on the reinforcements advancing from the Chippawa river. Half a century later he wrote in his memoirs, 'an extravagant opinion generally prevailed throughout the army in respect to the prowess – nay, invincibility of Scott's brigade.'

The ensuing battle began after seven o'clock, just half an hour before the sun was due to set. The earliest losses were almost exclusively American; the British and Canadian position and artillery gave their force a considerable advantage. Scott achieved success when he ordered the 25th United States Infantry to flank the enemy's left. The British and Canadians, caught in the midst of redeploying, where driven back temporarily. A more permanent and significant triumph came through the capture of Riall, who was caught as the 25th rode to the rear.

Riall's leadership was not missed. As the battle entered its second hour Drummond surveyed the field with considerable satisfaction, drawn in part from a mistaken belief that he had been waging war against the entire strength of Brown's invading army. Then, at approximately half past eight, Brown and the main body of Americans arrived from Chippawa.

The sides were now roughly even; more than 6,000 men were fighting in the darkness amid the smoke of artillery and muskets. It was, Brown reported, 'very difficult to distinguish at any considerable distance, the Hostile columns or Lines.'

Indeed, nightfall had added to the confusion and chaos of

the battlefield. Riall's capture had taken place when he had ridden towards what he took to be British troops. Before the end of battle, both sides would suffer casualties inflicted by their own; the Glengarry Fencibles would come under fire by British regulars.

In this dark atmosphere of smoke and shadow, some British officers managed simply to slip away from their American captors. The unfortunate Major General Riall was not among them. Wounded, he would eventually lose his right arm to amputation.

After Brown's arrival, a victory for the British and Canadians began to look less certain, and nearly evaporated when Brown ordered the capture of the British artillery. The task fell to the 21st United States Infantry under Lieutenant Colonel James Miller, a veteran of the Battle of Detroit. While the British and Canadians were fighting off an assault on their right, Miller's troops deployed just metres from the British artillery. Firing a volley, followed by a bayonet charge, the infantry killed nearly every British gunner. Drummond later reported: 'Of so determined a

Character were the American attacks directed against our guns that our Artillery Men were bayoneted by the enemy in the Act of loading, and the muzzles of the Enemy's Guns were advanced within a few Yards of ours'.

The lieutenant governor, now wounded himself, mounted three attempts to retake his own guns, but was beaten off.

As the fifth hour of battle was drawing to a close, the fighting ceased. This ending was not governed by formal arrangement, rather by exhaustion and injury. Through wounds or death, the British and Canadian force had lost nearly 900 men. American casualties were almost identical. Brown and Scott featured among the wounded; the latter, who had to withdraw from the campaign, would lose his left arm. Drummond, too, had been injured. As blood flowed from a wound to his neck, he watched as the Americans retreated.

Although the British and Canadians took possession of the battlefield, it was not until the next morning's dawn that the true extent of the carnage was revealed. A British Sergeant, James Commins, observed: 'The morning light ushered to our view a shocking spectacle, Americans and

English laid upon one another, occasioned by our advance and retreat. Nearly 2,000 was left on the field.'

Shortly thereafter, the American, Brigadier General Ripley, returned with all available men – a force of some 1,200 – but found the battlefield occupied by 2,200 British and Canadians. Ripley withdrew without incident – and continued to withdraw. Recognizing that they were no longer an effective force, the American army fell back to Fort Erie, destroying the old British fortifications along the Chippawa river and burning the King's Bridge.

Official British reports recorded 84 British and Canadian deaths. Brown wrote that 173 Americans died in the battle, a number many historians consider conservative.

In 1867, the year of Confederation, Alexander Muir penned 'The Maple Leaf Forever', the song which very nearly became Canada's national anthem. Muir, himself a veteran of the 1866 Battle of Ridgeway, the last to be fought on the Niagara frontier, recognized the two greatest conflicts of the War of 1812:

At Queenston Heights and Lundy's Lane
Our brave fathers, side by side,
For freedom, homes, and loved ones dear,
Firmly stood and nobly died;
And those dear rights which they maintained,
We swear to yield them never!
Our watchword evermore shall be,
The Maple Leaf forever!

The Battle of Lundy's Lane was the last major conflict of the war to be fought on Canadian soil. Five months later, on Christmas Eve, British and American diplomats in Ghent, Belgium, brought the war to an end. The Treaty of Ghent included no territorial concessions and ensured the return of all property seized. Tragically, news of the treaty took some time to reach all combatants, and on 8 January 1815, thousands were killed in the British defeat at the Battle of New Orleans.

CHAPTER V

—◆—

The Rebellions *of* 1837

THE STRUGGLE AGAINST THE ELITES
1837–8

An introduction

THE INHABITANTS OF the Canadas had refused all invitations to join the Thirteen Colonies in their revolution, and in the War of 1812 had fought off American attempts to impose their version of democracy and republicanism on British North America. And yet the two decades that had followed that last war had been marred by growing dissatisfaction with the political process.

The greatest source of this discontent was found in the fact that the popularly elected Legislative Assemblies of Lower and Upper Canada were ultimately under the control of established elites. In both provinces, elected reformers pushed for truly representative government. Anything but a united front, divisions hindered their progress. This was particularly true in Lower Canada, where anti-clerical reformers alienated those reformers within the Roman Catholic Church.

Of all the reformers in the province, the most prominent was the leader of the Parti Patriote, lawyer and seigneur Louis-Joseph Papineau. As the dominant party in the Legislative Assembly, in 1834 the Patriotes were responsible for the Ninety-Two Resolutions, a list of demands submitted to Westminster. It was the rejection of these resolutions three years later that sparked the fire of rebellion in Lower Canada and, ultimately, Upper Canada.

Like the 'War of 1812', the name 'Rebellions of 1837' is deceiving. In fact, the struggles in Canada continued throughout the year that followed. Led by Robert Nelson, Patriotes living in the United States staged two unsuccessful invasions that were focused on Lower Canada.

Upper Canada, too, was the target of attacks from American soil. With few exceptions, these invaders had not been participants in the rebel cause, rather they were Americans. A diverse group known as the Patriot Hunters, some wished Canada to be absorbed by the United States, some sought to establish a republic to the north, while a significant number took part as soldiers of fortune. In February, a large force was thwarted in an attempt to seize Pelée Island. This was followed by a June raid at Short Hills on the Niagara frontier, and autumn assaults at Windsor and at Windmill Point, just east of Prescott. Ill-planned and lacking any significant support within Upper Canada, all met with failure. In fact, the assaults from the United States served to strengthen the enemies of radical reform and made the policies of the moderate reformers appear sound. Faced with rebellion and raids across the border, the inhabitants of Upper Canada demonstrated a marked preference for existing British institutions.

Within three years of the failed rebellions, the two Canadas were united as the Province of Canada. The new political entity, which suffered under great instability, came to an end in 1867 with Confederation.

THE BATTLE *of* SAINT-DENIS

23 NOVEMBER 1837

———•·•———

AFTER THE REJECTION of their Ninety-Two Resolutions in March 1837, the Patriotes found themselves increasingly alienated and powerless. Much of the Legislative Assembly's power over the public purse had been stripped and, on 15 June, public meetings were declared illegal. The ban did nothing to prevent the Patriotes from rallying. The most important of these meetings took place on 23 October at Saint-Charles-sur-Richelieu, a two-day event billed as the Grand Assembly of the Six Counties – Richelieu, Saint-Hyathinthe, Rouville, Chambly, Verchères and L'Acadie. It was there that Louis-Joseph Papineau, leader of the Patriotes, called for his supporters to elect their own justices and militia officers – the first steps toward establishing a provisional government. Fellow Patriote Wolfred Nelson went much further, urging rebellion. 'I say that the time has come', he told the assembled crowd of 5,000, 'to melt down our dishes and tin spoons to make bullets.'

The response to Nelson, a Protestant medical doctor, came the next day in a pastoral letter written by Monseigneur Jean-Jacques Lartigue, the Bishop of Montreal:

> *Have you seriously thought about the horrors a civil war would bring? Have you imagined the rivers of blood flowing through the roads and countryside, and innocent people overwhelmed along with the guilty in the same series of disasters? Have you considered that every popular revolution, almost without exception, is a blood-letting?*

The effect of the bishop's letter was limited at best.

Two weeks later, the first skirmish took place in Montreal. Members of Les Fils de la Liberté, a paramilitary wing of the Patriotes, engaged in a street fight with a group of young Tories called the Doric Club. Four days later, the first shots were fired when Patriotes attacked a troop of militia at

Saint-Jean-sur-Richelieu. Threatened with arrest, Papineau and other leaders went into hiding.

On 18 November, Thomas Storrow Brown, a 'general' in Les Fils de la Liberté, established a rebel camp at the seized manoir of a seigneur just south of Saint-Charles-sur-Richelieu. The town, then flourishing through trade brought by the river, had become the centre of Patriote activity. Papineau and other leaders reappeared to meet and discuss strategy. The Patriotes moved throughout the Richelieu valley and the county of Deux-Montagnes, threatening justices, militia officers and others in authority who had not joined their side.

None of these actions escaped notice. At York, nearly 500 km to the west, Lieutenant Governor Sir Francis Bond Head ordered all regulars stationed in Upper Canada to Lower Canada. The force joined their fellow regulars in the eastern province under the command of General Sir John Colborne. In his 60th year, Colborne was considered a remarkable military strategist. He had for many years served under Wellington and was responsible for the defeat of Napoleon's Vielle Garde at Waterloo. In 1828, the general had assumed an appointment as lieutenant governor of Upper Canada. His service in British North America was somewhat less glorious than that he'd brought to the European theatre. As lieutenant governor he had demonstrated favouritism to British immigrants and had distributed funds against the wishes of the Legislative Assembly. In short, Colborne had contributed to the growing unrest in Upper Canada.

In January 1836, the general was replaced by Head, a supporter of moderate reform. Colborne had been preparing his return to Great Britain when the unrest in Lower Canada turned to violence.

The general argued that a pre-emptive strike was the best way to deal with Papineau and his Patriotes. He dispatched two detachments consisting of five companies each to Saint-Charles-sur-Richelieu and the village of Saint-Denis.

Throughout the evening of 23 November and into the morning of the next day, Colonel Charles Gore marched 300 regulars through the rain and cold of the countryside towards Saint-Denis. Three km outside of the village they were ambushed when a group of Patriotes ran out of a house and began firing from behind a barricade. Exposed, Gore's regulars quickly took up position behind a low stone wall.

Under the command of Nelson, the Patriotes proved to be a formidable and well-disciplined force. Composed primarily of local farmers and merchants, they were able to hold off the regulars. As the battle stretched into mid-afternoon, their numbers were increased to approximately 800 by the arrival of reinforcements.

The situation among the regulars was deteriorating. Exhausted from the overnight march, they found themselves running short of ammunition; no one had anticipated such resistance. Gore was forced to call a retreat to Sorel.

Although the Battle of Saint-Denis had lasted for six hours, casualties were surprisingly light. Six regulars and 12 Patriotes had been killed – more than the total number of wounded.

Missing from the Patriotes' victory celebration was their

leader Papineau. His absence has become the subject of debate. While some have claimed that Papineau fled, others have written that Nelson had sought to protect his leader, and so had asked the politician to leave the scene of battle.

Though the Patriote victory had been great, Nelson recognized that the battle would have enormous consequences. 'We have now passed the Rubicon', he wrote. 'Our very lives are at stake.'

THE BATTLE *of* SAINT-CHARLES
25 NOVEMBER 1837

————•◆•————

EARLY ON THE second morning after Wolfred Nelson's victory at the Battle of Saint-Denis, General Colborne's second dispatch, a force of 420 men under the command of Lieutenant Colonel George Wetherall, arrived at the rebel camp outside Saint-Charles-sur-Richelieu. It had been a week since Thomas Storrow Brown had seized the seigneurial manoir. In that seven days, his original force of 100 men had more than doubled in size.

As a leader, Brown was not of the same calibre as Nelson. Though he had knowledge of the Battle of Saint-Denis, and certainly must have realized his base was under threat, the 'general' had made few preparations for the arrival of the British regulars. This time there was no ambush; the Patriotes were on the defensive from the very start.

As Wetherall's men marched towards the manoir, the Patriotes took positions behind poorly constructed breastworks and began firing at the centre line. The lieutenant colonel's hope that his show of force would induce defection had not come to pass. Wetherall ordered his three centre companies to fix bayonets and charge. Covered by fire from the other regulars, the Royals, one of the British Army's most hardened regiments, advanced on the Patriote barricade, forcing the rebels back to the freezing waters of the Richelieu river.

This unequal contest ended in slaughter.

At the water's edge, the Patriotes fell to their knees and placed their rifles upside down as if in surrender. But just as the Royals approached, they took their arms in hand and fired. The only surviving account of the Royals' reaction is provided in a memoir written by Lieutenant Charles Beauclerk: 'This act of treachery caused, until restrained by the officers, a general massacre; which, while it lasted, was indeed dreadful.'

Three British regulars were killed in this, the second battle of the rebellion. It is believed that 150 Patriotes died, some as they attempted to escape by swimming the cold waters of the Richelieu.

THE BATTLE *of* MONTGOMERY'S TAVERN
7 DECEMBER 1837

────◆────

Had THERE NOT been an uprising in Lower Canada, it is unlikely that any Upper Canadian revolt would have taken place. Discontent with the political system had sown fewer seeds of rebellion. This is reflected in the battle that took place at Montgomery's Tavern, a clash that is sometimes described, somewhat dismissively, as 'The Bar Fight on Yonge Street'.

The leader of the bar fight was William Lyon Mackenzie, the most influential and radical among the reformers of Upper Canada. An immigrant from Scotland, he was publisher of the *Colonial Advocate*, through which he took on the elites and argued for political reform. Mackenzie was a divisive though popular figure, managing to win election to the Legislative Assembly of Upper Canada and later serving as the first mayor of Toronto. However, Mackenzie seemed incapable of transforming his success at the ballot box into meaningful change. Whether radical or moderate, the reformers of Upper Canada made no significant progress, and in the election of July 1836, Mackenzie lost his seat.

After his electoral defeat, Mackenzie began a new newspaper, the aptly named *Constitution*, in which he promoted wholescale constitutional reform. By the summer of 1837, however, he had replaced reform with revolution. He was elected secretary of an organization called the Committee of Vigilance of Upper Canada, an organization which adopted an American-modelled Declaration of Independence.

In the autumn of 1837, when rebellion broke out in Lower Canada and Lieutenant Governor Sir Francis Bond Head dispatched York's British regulars to Lower Canada, Mackenzie saw it was his time to act. Through a combination of pressure and false information, he obtained the support of fellow reformers John Rolph and Thomas David Morrison for a revolt which would begin on 7 December. It was Mackenzie's belief that the revolution could be successfully carried to fruition without violence; he believed that a simple show of force would bring about the collapse of the government.

Five days before the revolution was to begin, Mackenzie met with supporters in Stoufville. When he returned to York he discovered that Rolph, having heard a false rumour, had ordered an early march on York. Rebels had begun to gather at the point of rendezvous, Montgomery's Tavern, some 8 km north of the city. Mackenzie was adamant that the rebellion stick to his schedule. Rather than lead the rebels to York, he chose to use them for reconnaissance. This scouting expedition ended in the death of a Colonel Robert Moodie, an elderly, retired military man, who was shot as he attempted to run a rebel roadblock.

The revolt having claimed its first victim, the following day Mackenzie became increasingly erratic. Where he previously considered the date of the rebellion as fixed, Rolph convinced the rebel leader to immediately begin the march on York.

In the late afternoon of 5 December, approximately 1,000

rebels armed with rifles, staves and pitchforks began marching south on Yonge Street. They were spotted by 27 loyalists who opened fire before fleeing towards the town. The front line of rebels returned fire and then dropped to the ground. In the fading autumn light, it appeared to those marching behind that every one of their brothers-in-arms in the front line had been killed. All turned and ran, thus ending not only the greatest battle of the Upper Canadian rebellion, but the most serious attempt to seize power. Though the skirmish was brief, two rebels and one loyalist were killed.

Dejected and depressed, Mackenzie returned to Montgomery's Tavern. 'This was almost too much for human patience', he later wrote. 'The city would have been ours in an hour, probably without firing a shot. But 800 ran, and unfortunately the wrong way.'

The rebel leader seemed incapable of action.

Two days later, those rebels that remained at Montgomery's Tavern, some 400 in total, were dispersed by a force of more than 1,000 armed loyalists.

Montgomery's Tavern was looted and burned to the ground.

Mackenzie escaped to the United States, where he received support from a number of Americans looking to liberate the Canadas from British rule. He selected as his new commander Rensselaer Van Rensselaer, a failed West Point student and the nephew of General Stephen Van Rensselaer, who 25 years earlier had failed so gloriously at the Battle of Queenston Heights.

On 13 December, Mackenzie returned with two dozen followers and Van Rensselaer to seize the unoccupied Navy Island, in the Niagara river. It was on this small body of land, located just above Niagara Falls, that he proclaimed the Republic of Canada. Heavily influenced by the flags of the American Revolution, the tricolour of this new state, designed by Mackenzie himself, featured two five-pointed stars, representing Upper and Lower Canada, above the word 'LIBERTY'.

From his island state, 'Chairman Pro. Tem.' Mackenzie issued a proclamation in which he promised $100 in silver and 300 acres (121 hectares) of 'the most valuable Lands in Canada' to each volunteer who would join his struggle.

Protests from Upper Canada were ignored by Washington as hundreds of American men, most of them suffering from seasonal unemployment, made their way to the seat of Mackenzie's provisional government. They were transported to the island by the Patriot Hunter supply ship the *Caroline*. Armed and manned, the Republic of Canada began to fire on the shore at Chippewa. And yet, Head refused the call to attack the island. He feared that an attack on American citizens, though on Canadian territory, would draw British North America into another war with the United States.

Early on the morning of 30 December, Colonel Allan McNab, whose argument for attack Head had snubbed, broke the impasse. Acting on the colonel's orders, Commander Andrew Drew, a veteran of the Napoleonic Wars, crossed into American waters and cut the *Caroline* loose from its moorings on the shore of New York State. Set ablaze, the empty supply ship sank. A few charred remnants were seen drifting over the falls.

On 13 January 1838, while under attack from British

armaments, Mackenzie again fled for the United States. He was arrested and charged with 'setting on foot a military enterprise at Buffalo, to be carried on against Upper Canada, a part of the Queen's dominions, at a time when the United States were at peace with Her Majesty; with having provided the means for the prosecution of the expedition; and with having done all this within the dominion and territory of the United States.' He was fined $10 and served 18 months in prison.

Mackenzie remained in the United States after his release, living in exile as a journalist and newspaper publisher. Receiving amnesty, in 1850 he returned to Canada and a year later was elected to Parliament. He died in 1861 of an apoplectic seizure.

This complex man, who had once expressed enthusiastic support for what he perceived as an obvious American desire to annex Upper Canada, did not live to see the birth of the grandson who would bear his name. William Lyon Mackenzie King went on to become the longest-serving prime minister in Canadian history.

THE BATTLE *of* SAINT-EUSTACHE
14 DECEMBER 1837

———•———

THE LAST GREAT conflict of the Lower Canada Rebellion, the Battle of Saint-Eustache was preceded by the establishment of rebel camps to the north of Montreal. It was from these bases that Patriote leaders Jean-Olivier Chénier and Amury Girod intended to seize the city. The strategy was a bold one. A little more than two decades earlier, thousands of American soldiers had held the same goal, yet had got no closer than the Châteauguay river and Crysler's Farm.

While the Patriotes may have been relying – perhaps too much – on sympathizers within the city, their cause was suffering from an absence of leadership. Louis-Joseph Papineau, Thomas Storrow Brown and Wolfred Nelson had fled to the United States, along with hundreds of other Patriotes. South of the border, the group had begun to fracture, owing to disagreements between Papineau and the more radical Nelson.

On 6 December, the Patriotes suffered another setback when 80 of their exiled number were ambushed by local militia as they attempted to re-enter Lower Canada from Vermont. One Patriote was killed, while arms, artillery, ammunition and four rebels were captured. The remaining Patriotes were again forced to flee to the United States.

By this time, William Henry Scott, one of the remaining Patriote leaders, had concluded that further military efforts would be futile and fatal. He encouraged Chénier and Girod to disband the northern camps, but was dismissed. Armed struggle had become inevitable.

Like Nelson, Chénier was a medical doctor – a man with no military experience. It was his great misfortune that he had as his opponent General John Colborne. However, even without the veteran of Waterloo, it is difficult to imagine how Chénier could have achieved a victory against the force with which he was confronted.

On 14 December, 1,200 regulars and 200 volunteers

marched slowly into the village of Saint-Eustache. Witnessing the display of force, many Patriotes fled; this was just the reaction Charles Gore had hoped for at Saint-Charles-sur-Richelieu. However, Chénier and approximately 250 other rebels remained. They holed themselves up in the village church, the convent and the presbytery, all of which they used as fortifications from which to fire upon the advancing British. As the parish priest, Father Jacques Paquin, looked on, Colborne ordered his artillery to fire upon the church. The bombardment lasted two hours, yet the church withstood all.

As dusk descended, a detachment of Royals entered the church in an attempt to drive the Patriotes out into the open. Once inside they fell victim to the Patriotes who were firing from the second storey. The staircases having been broken down, the Royals were forced to withdraw. However, before abandoning the church, they set the altar cloth alight. Before long, the rebels were jumping from the windows. Paquin, who had opposed the rebellion, described Chénier's final moments:

Dr. Chénier, seeing all hope had been lost and he could not dream of defending himself within the church, which was now ablaze, brought some of his men together and jumped with them through the windows on the convent side. He wanted to escape but he could not get out of the cemetery, and soon was caught by a bullet, dropped to the ground and died almost immediately.

The end of the Battle of Saint-Eustache came quickly, with little mercy shown to the remaining Patriotes. In the end, three British regulars lost their lives. The number of Patriote fatalities was something approaching 100.

Among the rebel survivors was Girod. Just as the fighting had begun, he left Saint-Eustache, supposedly to obtain Patriotes from Saint-Benoît. As these reinforcements never arrived, Girod was accused of cowardice. He eventually committed suicide.

The following day, Colborne and his troops entered Saint-Benoît, where they found the Patriote camp in a state of disarray. There was no need for battle as the rebels had fled. The village was summarily burned to the ground. From Saint-Benoît, Colborne's men moved on to Saint-Joachim, Sainte-Scholastique and Sainte-Thérèse, torching the houses of the rebel leaders, and rounding up Patriotes.

During the next two years, hundreds of Patriotes were tried for the crime of high treason. Twelve men were hanged, while more than 100 others were sent to the penal colony of Australia. This second sentence inspired '*Un Canadien errant*':

> *Un Canadien errant,*
> *Banni de ses foyers,*
> *Parcourait en pleurant*
> *Des pays étrangers.*
> *Un jour, triste et pensif,*
> *Assis au bord des flots,*
> *Au courant fugitif*
> *Il adressa ces mots*
> *"Si tu vois mon pays,*

Mon pays malheureux,
Va, dis à mes amis
Que je me souviens d'eux.
"O jours si pleins d'appas
Vous êtes disparus,
Et ma patrie, hélas!
Je ne la verrai plus!
"Non, mais en expirant,
O mon cher Canada!
Mon regard languissant
Vers toi se portera"

Wolfred Nelson, who had returned from the United States, was sentenced to exile in Bermuda with seven other Patriotes. His brother, Robert Nelson, became the leader of the Frères chasseurs. Intent on continuing the rebellion, their only act of significance was a raid on the seigneurial manoir and village of Beauharnois.

Papineau remained safe in the United States, where he lived until 1844, when he was granted amnesty. He returned to his seigneury, and in 1848 re-entered politics. A firm opponent of the Act of Union, the former leader of the Patriotes became an advocate of annexation to the United States.

THE BATTLE *of* THE WINDMILL
12–16 NOVEMBER 1838

O F ALL THE incursions into the Canadas by the Frères chasseurs and the Patriot Hunters, the largest by far was that which resulted in the Battle of the Windmill. The theatre of war, Windmill Point, was not the intended location, nor did the reception meet expectations.

Although membership in the Hunters' Lodges was overwhelmingly American, the Patriot Hunters recruited Nils Von Schoultz, a Finnish-born Swedish national, to lead their November assault. It was believed that the 31-year-old Von Schoultz, a former officer in the Polish Army, would provide the knowledge and experience, lacking in previous attempts, to establish a foothold from which the Rebellion of Upper Canada could be reignited.

While Von Schoultz's role involved planning and giving advice, overall military command fell to his recruiter, a senior member of the Hunters' Lodge named John Ward

Birge. The naval operation was under the authority of Bill Johnston, one of only a handful of Canadians involved in the campaign. A criminal, Johnston had been supporting himself through piracy on the Saint Lawrence river and Lake Ontario.

The Patriot Hunters' target was Prescott, a place Johnston knew well. A small town on the north shore of the Saint Lawrence river, it was the site of Fort Wellington, a British military fortification which served as a depot for the Upper Canadian militia.

In preparation for the assault, the Patriot Hunters gathered at Sackets Harbor, New York. On 11 November, they sailed down the river to Ogdensburg, an American town directly across the river from their Canadian target. Early the next morning, roughly 250 Patriot Hunters on two vessels attempted to land at Prescott, but were fought off by the town's militia. Unable to disembark, the force remained on their craft, which then ran aground on a mud flat near Ogdensburg. There they remained until Johnston managed to free the vessels.

Thwarted by the local militia and very nearly defeated by the mud flats, the Patriot Hunters set their sights on a new target: Newport, 3 km to the east of Prescott. As a hamlet, the community had no means by which they could resist an invading force.

While the Patriot Hunters had failed to seize Prescott and Fort Wellington, Newport was not lacking in tactical significance. For the most part, it consisted of structures built of limestone. In recent years, the surrounding land had been cleared of trees and now featured a series of field-stone and wood fences intended for livestock. The hamlet itself was located on a point which jutted out into the Saint Lawrence. Strong currents and a 30-ft bluff provided an advantage over any force attempting an assault by water.

Ultimately, Newport's greatest feature was a large 60-ft windmill constructed of thick stone. Sitting on the 30-ft bluff, the structure offered a panoramic view which, it was thought, would have great value in the Patriot Hunters' campaign. Indeed, it was no surprise when 600 Upper Canadian militiamen, supported by several British infantry units from the 83rd Regiment, attempted to take back Newport and its windmill shortly after dawn the next morning. While losses were suffered due to the Patriot Hunters' firing from the protection of the hamlet's limestone buildings, the militiamen managed to take back Newport. The Patriot Hunters were driven back, seeking protection in the windmill. The structure proved an ideal fortification, easily withstanding the fire of small arms and field artillery. By the time the militia commanders realized the futility of their assault and withdrew, 13 of their men had been killed, with a further 70 wounded. Losses among the Patriot Hunters were also great: 18 dead and an unknown number wounded.

With the Patriot Hunters now holed up in the windmill there followed two days of stand-off. Von Schoultz could see ships of the Royal Navy and the United States Navy patrolling the Saint Lawrence. Prior to the battle, Birge and Johnston had withdrawn to Ogdensberg for supplies and reinforcements. It was evident to Von Schoultz that the pair would not be returning. Though he could not have known it, senior Patriot Hunter leaders had fled the town to avoid arrest. Von Schoultz and the men under his command had been abandoned. He could do little more than watch as the Royal Artillery brought in an 18-pounder (8-kg) battery from Kingston.

On 16 November, a second assault on the windmill began with an artillery bombardment, supported by more than 1,600 British regulars and Canadian militia. Within the structure, casualties quickly began to mount. With only a single exit, the invaders' fortress had become a death-trap; Von Schoultz had no choice but to surrender unconditionally. When the battle ended, a further 35 of his men had been killed. The British and Canadians suffered no losses.

Though the windmill was surrounded and Royal Navy gunboats and steamers cut off any chance of crossing into the United States, a small number of Patriot Hunters managed to escape. Von Schoultz was not one of these fortunate few. He joined the prisoners transported to Kingston for trial. There, legal counsel was provided by John A. Macdonald, the young lawyer who within three decades would become the first Prime Minister of the Dominion of Canada.

When he took the stand, Von Schoultz told the court that he believed he should be made to pay for his crimes, a statement Macdonald advised against. Of the 197 Patriot Hunters taken prisoner, he was the only one of the captives to plead guilty to violations of law. Von Schoultz maintained that he been misinformed as to the true desires and aspirations of Upper Canadians. This regret won the recruited Patriot Hunter the support of several prominent citizens, some of whom wrote to Lieutenant Governor Sir George Arthur pleading that his life be spared.

In the end, Von Schoultz and ten of his fellow Patriot Hunters were sentenced to death. He was hanged in a private execution at Fort Henry on 8 December.

Forty of the remaining captives were acquitted, while 86 received pardons. A further 60 were sentenced to penal transportation to Australia.

After the assault on Newport, the Hunters' Lodges were outlawed by American President Martin Van Buren.

The Patriot Hunters managed only one last rai[...] significance. A few weeks after the Battle of the Wind[...]ll, 25 of their number were killed in a raid on Windsor. Although much property was destroyed, there were no Canadian fatalities.

CHAPTER VI

—◆—

The Fenian Raids

THE IRISH INVASION *of* CANADA
1866–71

An introduction

WITH HINDSIGHT THE Fenian Raids may appear to be mere skirmishes worthy of little more than a footnote in the grand scheme of history. They were, after all, minor battles with few casualties, fought for reasons that today appear at once bizarre and impossible. However, these attacks were once considered grave threats to the survival of British North America and, later, the Dominion of Canada. Although it cannot be claimed that confederation was a consequence of the Fenian activity, the threat from the south served to support the argument put forth by Sir John A. Macdonald and others that the defence of British North

America would be strengthened through colonial union.

The enemy in battle was not a the army of another country, but members of a secret fraternal organization, the Fenian Brotherhood, based in New York City. Established by Irish immigrants in the mid-18th century, the Fenians believed that the capture of Canada would lead to an independent Ireland. They were certain that such an invasion would lead to one of two scenarios. The first had the Crown offering a free Ireland in exchange for an end to Fenian occupation; in the second, a great number of British troops would be sent to liberate the North American colonies, allowing for a successful uprising on the Emerald Isle.

The role of the United States government in the Fenian Raids has been a subject of debate. The American Civil War, which ended the year before the first raid, had produced a period of great tension between the United States and British North America. Confederate agents had operated in the Canadas and in 1864 had launched an assault against the border town of Saint Albans, Vermont.

During the months leading to the first Fenian Raid,

American President Andrew Johnson had met with leaders of the brotherhood. It was reported that when asked about a possible Fenian seizure of British territory in North America, the president had responded that he would recognize 'accomplished facts'.

Most of the Fenians who took part in 'the Irish Invasion of Canada' were hardened veterans of the American Civil War. Indeed, those who fought often augmented their civilian dress with articles taken from Union and Confederate uniforms. Nevertheless, nearly all of the raids were successfully repelled by local volunteer militias comprised of men with little or no training.

THE BATTLE *of* RIDGEWAY
2 JUNE 1866

———•———

THE FENIAN BROTHERHOOD had intended as its first seizure New Brunswick's Campobello Island, located within the Bay of Fundy at the entrance to Passamaquoddy Bay. Beginning early in April 1866, a force of 1,000 men began assembling in the north-east of Maine. All was poorly planned. The supposed invaders arrived weeks ahead of their arms, which were scheduled to arrive mid-month by steamer from New York. The presence of so many Irish-American strangers – including some 400 in the small Maine town of Eastport – did not escape notice. Supported by regulars, 5,000 men of New Brunswick's volunteer militia established a chain of posts along the Saint Croix river and six British warships were dispatched to the area.

In the end, the raid was thwarted not by the British, nor by the colonial militia, but by a force of 700 American soldiers. Under the command of General George Meade, the victor over Robert E. Lee at the Battle of Gettysburg, the troops dispersed the Fenians before the raid could be launched. Campobello Island was never touched, few shots were fired and there were no casualties. The damage suffered by New Brunswick was limited to the burning of four small buildings and the loss of a Union Jack, results of two separate assaults on nearby Indian Island.

The events that took place at Ridgeway were markedly different. The ill-fated Campobello Island campaign, which had come to be known as the 'Eastport Fizzle', had prompted complacency in some quarters. The Fenian Brotherhood, though still considered a threat, had shown itself to be ill prepared and its leadership incompetent. In retrospect, the arrival of the six warships was seen as a great overreaction. Finally, Meade's intervention had lent the impression that the American government would not permit any raid from its territory.

Complacency was joined by bold presumption. On 22 May 1866, a mere month after the scattering of the Campobello Island raiders, the British Consul in Buffalo, H.W. Hemans, wrote that Fenianism was all but dead. Yet, four days after his declaration, the consul received evidence of a planned attack on the Niagara frontier. Where the arrival of the first Fenians had gone unnoticed in Buffalo's large Irish-American population, their swelling number now led to reports of 'many strange military men'. One Canadian agent described the city as being 'full of Fenians'. Another agent reported that 1,000 Fenians were en route from Cleveland.

By the month's end, the once complacent Canadians were now alarmed. This time the British warships and border defences were non-existent. As armed Fenians amassed in Buffalo, American authorities stood aside, determined to let the 'wild and absurd project die a natural death'. The defence of Canada West was left to untrained local militias.

In the early hours of 1 June, well before dawn, more than 800 Fenian soldiers crossed the Niagara river and landed on Canadian soil. Calling themselves the 'Irish Republican Army', the earliest group to use the name, they were under the command of Irish immigrant John O'Neill, who had served as a former Union cavalry officer under General

William Tecumseh Sherman. O'Neill's IRA encountered no resistance. In fact, the only obstacle encountered by his men came in the form of the USS *Michigan*, an iron-hulled warship, which arrived after the campaign had begun. As a result, an unknown number of Fenians – probably numbering several hundred – were prevented from crossing the Niagara.

O'Neill's men seized the town of Fort Erie, cut the telegraph wires, tore up train tracks and set fire to a railway bridge. After seizing horses and demanding to be fed by the citizens of the town, the Fenians set up camp on a farm 7 km to the north. Several men were sent out as scouts, while others were charged with distributing a proclamation issued by Thomas W. 'Fighting Tom' Sweeny, 'Major General Commanding the Armies of Ireland', from the Brotherhood's headquarters in Manhattan:

> *To the People of British America:*
> *We come among you as the foes of British rule in Ireland.*
> *We have taken up the sword to strike down the oppressors'*

rod, to deliver Ireland from the tyrant, the despoiler, the robber. We have registered our oaths upon the altar of our country in the full view of heaven and sent up our vows to the throne of Him who inspired them. Then, looking about us for an enemy, we find him here, here in your midst, where he is most vulnerable and convenient to our strength ... We have no issue with the people of these Provinces, and wish to have none but the most friendly relations. Our weapons are for the oppressors of Ireland. Our bows shall be directed only against the power of England; her privileges alone shall we invade, not yours. We do not propose to divest you of a solitary right you now enjoy ... We are here neither as murderers, nor robbers, for plunder and spoliation. We are here as the Irish army of liberation, the friends of liberty against despotism, of democracy against aristocracy, of the people against their oppressors. In a word, our war is with the armed power of England, not with the people, not with these Provinces. Against England, upon land and sea, till Ireland is free ... To Irishmen throughout these Provinces we appeal in the name of seven centuries of British iniquity and Irish misery and suffering, in the names of our murdered sires, our desolate homes, our desecrated altars, our million of famine graves, our insulted name and race — to stretch forth the hand of brotherhood in the holy cause of fatherland, and smite the tyrant where we can. We conjure you, our countrymen, who from misfortune inflicted by the very tyranny you are serving, or from any other cause, have been forced to enter the ranks of the enemy, not to be willing instruments of your country's death or degradation. No uniform, and surely not the blood-dyed coat of England, can emancipate you from the natural law that binds your allegiance to Ireland, to liberty, to right, to justice. To the friends of Ireland, of freedom, of humanity, of the people, we offer the olive branch of peace and the honest grasp of friendship. Take it Irishmen, Frenchmen, American, take it all and trust it ... We wish to meet with friends; we are prepared to meet with enemies. We shall endeavor to merit the confidence of the former, and the latter can expect from us but the leniency of a determined though generous foe and the restraints and relations imposed by civilized warfare.

Whatever the expectations of the brotherhood, O'Neill's force met no friends, nor did they meet with enemies. The Canadian response to news of Fenians amassing in Buffalo had been slow. Indeed, there had been no calling out of militia units until after the invasion had begun. Operations against O'Neill's IRA effectively fell to Major General George Napier, the commander of British soldiers in Canada West. His first objective was the securing of the Welland Canal, which linked Lake Erie and Lake Ontario, allowing ships to bypass Niagara Falls. This was easily accomplished as O'Neill had his men preparing for battle some 26 km to the east. The northern entrance of the canal, at Port Dalhousie, was secured by men under the command of Colonel George Peacocke, while others under Lieutenant Colonel Alfred Booker secured the southern entrance at Port Colborne.

Neither man could claim great experience in dealing with the Civil War veteran O'Neill. A British officer, Peacocke had never commanded in action; Booker, despite his 11 years in the militia, had not only never commanded a unit, he had also never experienced enemy gunfire.

Peacocke's plan was to march his force of 1,700 men – comprised of the Queen's Own Rifles, the 2nd and 13th Battalions, the Volunteer Militia Infantry of Hamilton, the Caledonia Rifles and the York Rifles – south to Stevensville, 8 km west of where the Fenians were encamped. Booker and his force of 850 militiamen were to proceed by train to Ridgeway, then on foot to meet those under Peacocke's command. There they would unite and confront the Fenian invaders.

However, Peacocke set out late and took a meandering route, which only served to tire his forces. Booker, on the other hand, remained true to the plan. Early on the morning of 2 June, he and his men disembarked at the Ridgeway train station and began what they thought would be an 8-km march north to Stevensville.

Thanks to the good work of his scouts, O'Neill was well aware of the activity among the Canadians and British. Determined to avoid battle with a combined force, he had marched his men south-west down the Lime Ridge Road. The Fenians were 3 km north of Ridgeway when they heard the whistle of Booker's locomotive, followed by the sound of bugles. It was a lucky break, allowing for enough time to throw up barricades and position themselves on the ridge overlooking the road.

Thus it was at 8:00, in the 29th hour of their campaign, that the Fenians at last encountered a military presence. Ambushed, the militiamen advanced towards the enemy barricade until a report was raised of an approaching Fenian cavalry. In fact, the raiders had no cavalry; the information came from militiamen who had spotted Fenian scouts on horseback. Chaos, confusion and contradiction ensued. Although many militia units carried on the advance, several retreated, and still others formed squares in preparation to repel the non-existent cavalry. After two hours of battle, Booker sounded a general retreat. He had lost 10 killed and

57 wounded. The Fenians had also suffered 10 killed; the number of their wounded is unknown.

Booker's men made their way south-west to the railway and followed the tracks until they met a locomotive, while the Fenians rested before returning to Fort Erie. There, O'Neill's men encountered a small group of Canadian militia.

Under the command of Lieutenant Colonel John Stroughton Dennis, a surveyor, these inexperienced men – fewer than 100 in number – had requisitioned the tugboat *W.T. Robb* and had sailed from Port Colborne to Black Creek with the goal of heading off an anticipated Fenian retreat. The militiamen had arrived at their destination as the Battle of Ridgeway was being fought. With no enemy in sight and the Fenians having apparently decamped, Dennis decided to sail south and dock at Fort Erie. The lieutenant colonel landed 70 of his men. He had expected to meet only a few fleeing Fenians, likely under close pursuit by Booker's men; instead he encountered a victorious IRA, nearly ten times greater than his force.

This second engagement, the Battle of Fort Erie, fought within the streets of the town, was a particularly bloody confrontation. Though the fighting lasted no more than half an hour, four Fenians were killed and ten injured. The Canadians retreated, casting off the tugboat and returning to Port Colborne.

Left behind, Dennis fled to the farmhouse of a friend, where he disguised himself as a labourer.

O'Neill once again had possession of Fort Erie; however, he was well aware of Peacocke's men converging from the north. Moreover, the presence of the USS *Michigan*, patrolling the Niagara river, ensured that no reinforcement was possible. After nightfall, he ordered a retreat back to the United States. While many Fenians chose to desert, crossing the Niagara with the aid of logs, rafts and stolen boats, most joined O'Neill in crossing together in the early hours of 3 June. They were soon intercepted by a United States Navy tugboat, and surrendered to American naval personnel.

Two days later, a headline on the front page of the *New York Times* proclaimed 'The Fenian Folly'. The accompanying news story, dateline Buffalo, began: 'The Fenian excitement here is rapidly subsiding, the so-called invasion having proved so ridiculous a failure.' And yet the Fenians had been victorious; the Battle of Ridgeway had been the first Irish victory over British forces since they had fought beside the French in the 1745 Battle of Fontenoy.

THE BATTLE *of* ECCLES HILL
25 MAY 1870

THE NIAGARA CAMPAIGN of 1866 had been intended as one of a number of simultaneous raids into Canada. Indeed, on 7 June, four days after John O'Neill's retreat from Fort Erie, 1,800 Fenians launched a raid from Saint Albans, Vermont, capturing the border villages of Frelighsburg and Saint Armand in Canada East. Although the intended goal was the securing of Montreal, some 80 km north-west, the raiders progressed no further. Instead they remained in the area, awaiting the arrival of 1,200 reinforcements – a force which, in all probability, never existed. As in the aborted raid on Campobello Island, Fenian aspirations fell victim to poor planning. Their supply line from Saint Albans, which had proved inadequate, came to an abrupt end through seizure by American authorities. On 9 June, after Frelighsburg and Saint Armand had been plundered, Fenian commander Samuel B. Spiers ordered his men to withdraw to the United States. Two hundred Fenians defied the order, but were soon driven off by local volunteers, including a cavalry unit composed of members of the Montreal Hunt Club. The only casualty of this minor skirmish, sometimes referred to as the Battle of Pigeon Hill, was a Canadian farmwoman who had been caught in the crossfire between the two forces.

Back in the United States, Spiers escaped arrest. His comrade O'Neill had not been so lucky. Held in Buffalo, he was eventually released on a $500 bond. There was never any trial.

Four years later, Spiers returned to the area of his aborted raid – this time under the command of O'Neill.

Much had changed since the battles of Ridgeway, Fort Erie and Pigeon Hill. The eastern border colonies of British North America had united to create the Dominion of Canada. As the young nation emerged and Britain had begun a withdrawal of its forces, Ottawa, in turn, passed the Militia Act of 1868, which provided for the establishment and training of a 40,000-man force. The antiquated muzzle-loading rifles used in the battles of 1866 were replaced with a variety of modern weaponry purchased in Great Britain and the United States. The farmers of Frelighsburg and Saint Armand, who had lost much property during Spiers' raid, took it upon themselves to purchase 40 Ballard sporting rifles for the expressed purpose of defending themselves against Irish and Irish-American raiders.

On the other side of the border, O'Neill had risen to the presidency of the Fenian Brotherhood. Yet all was not well. Though it had the victor of the Niagara campaign at its helm, the organization had become fractious, quarrelsome and directionless. It appears likely that O'Neill's 1870 military campaign was designed to unite his weakening brotherhood.

At his base in Franklin, Vermont, a small town not 3 km from the Canadian border, O'Neill amassed 15,000 weapons, 3,000,000 rounds of ammunition and a piece of field artillery. Clearly, his expectations were high. Indeed, there is some speculation that this president of the Fenian Brotherhood had intended to capture Montreal, the very same goal that had so easily eluded Spiers. Whether true or not, disappointment must have been great as fewer than 400 Fenians reported for O'Neill's second invasion of Canada. Nevertheless, on the morning of 25 May, the invading party set out for the border.

Trouble for the Fenians began at noon, just after their advance guard crossed into Canada. Marching in close ranks, they came under fire from local farmers and the Missiquoi Home Guard, who both occupied the strategic heights of Eccles Hill. While some of the invaders fled for cover, others retreated the very short distance to the United States. It was there, just south of the border, that O'Neill was arrested by marshals.

For O'Neill, the contrast between the Battle of Ridgeway and what would become known as the Battle of Eccles Hill was great. In the Niagara, twenty-eight hours had elapsed before he had encountered a Canadian force; the first shots in this invasion had been fired within a matter of minutes. While some measure of the difference is explained by the proactive measures taken by the inhabitants of Frelighsburg and Saint Armand, it is best explained by the actions of Lieutenant Colonel William Osborne Smith. A Welsh-Canadian career army officer, Smith had been well aware of the flurry of Fenian activity and had positioned local militia units along the border.

Two hours into the Battle of Eccles Hill, the Montreal Troop of Cavalry and the 3rd Victoria Rifles arrived to bolster Canadian defences. Now under the command of Spiers, the invaders from the south had been strengthened by 100 members of the 4th New York Fenian Regiment.

As the battle was reaching the end of its sixth hour, Smith learned that field artillery was being brought up from Franklin. Taking the initiative, he positioned the Victoria Rifles on high ground and ordered the Missiquoi Battalion to lead a charge. The overwhelming show of force caused the invaders to flee for the border. Four dead comrades were left in their wake; a fifth Fenian, Captain E. Corman, a veteran of the American Civil War, died of his wounds several days later. No Canadians were harmed.

The Battle of Eccles Hill holds a place in Canadian

history as the first attempt at an invasion of the Dominion of Canada. Coming less than three years after Confederation, it demonstrated that the young country had learned much from the raids of 1866 and was capable of defending itself.

O'Neill's failure at Eccles Hill was not the final Fenian raid. A smaller, simultaneous raid had taken place south of Huntingdon, Quebec, 100 km to the west. Breastworks had been erected and rifle pits dug before news of the defeat caused the Fenians to retreat to the United States. Two days later, they returned under cover of night, but were easily beaten back by Canadian militia, who killed three Fenians. Again, no Canadians were harmed.

For his violation of neutrality laws, O'Neill received a sentence of six months. Though the Fenian Brotherhood gradually fell to pieces, its president continued to press for an invasion of Canada. After his release from prison, O'Neill travelled to Saint Paul, Minnesota, where he planned one more raid. This man, an American Civil War veteran, who had once commanded 800 members of the first Irish

Republican Army, was reduced to a force of just 40 men. O'Neill was convinced that this, his third invasion, would receive Métis support, leading to some sort of uprising; however Louis Riel, the Métis leader, would have nothing to do with the plans of the Fenians. On 5 October 1871, the force of 40 raided the Pembina Hudson Bay Post in Manitoba, and marched 20 prisoners back to the United States. It wasn't until the following day that Canadian authorities learned of the 'invasion', by which time the Fenians had been arrested by members of the United States Army.

O'Neill's third invasion of Canada proved to be his last. He died six years later in Nebraska. The Fenian Brotherhood outlived its greatest hero, but only just. By the dawn of the 20th century, the Fenian raids were all but forgotten. In 1910, one veteran of the raids, the remarkably named John A. Macdonald, bemoaned:

> *The people of the present generation know very little of the Fenian troubles of 1866 and 1870, and the great mass of the young Canadian boys and girls who are being*

educated in our Public Schools and Colleges are in total ignorance of the grave danger which cast dark shadows over this fair and prosperous Dominion in those stormy days. It was a period of great peril to this rising young Nation of the North, which might possibly have ended in the severance of Canada from British dominion. But happily this was prevented by the prompt measures that were taken to defend our soil, and the quick response that was made by the resolute Canadian Volunteers when the bugles sounded the call to assemble for active service on our frontiers.

CHAPTER VII

The North-West Rebellion

THE WAR *on the* PRAIRIES
1885
An introduction

THE NORTH-WEST Rebellion is frequently confused with the earlier Red River Rebellion; indeed it is not too unusual to see them referred to mistakenly as one and the same. They were, in fact, separated by more than 16 years and 800 km. Nevertheless, the two rebellions had much in common; both involved struggles for land, both centred on conflict between the Métis and Ottawa and both were led by the tragic figure of Louis Riel.

The seeds of the rebellions were sown in 1868 when Canada purchased Rupert's Land from the Hudson's Bay Company. Transfer of this massive acquisition was delayed by the resistance of the Métis and other inhabitants of the Red River Settlement. On 8 December 1869, a provisional government was established. Soon led by Riel, this 'Provisional Government of Rupert's Land and the Northwest Territory' first declared independence, then began negotiations for entry into the Dominion.

In Ottawa, there had been some sympathy. Prime Minister John A. Macdonald wrote: 'No explanation it appears has been made of the arrangement by which the country is to be handed over. All these people know is that Canada has bought the country from the Hudson's Bay Company and that they are handed over like a flock of sheep to us.' However, with Riel's obstruction impeding progress, the mood became increasingly hostile. Macdonald was soon calling for the 'impulsive half-breeds' to be 'kept down by a strong hand, until they are swamped by an influx of settlers.' And yet, he attempted to conciliate Riel's government by sending a delegation with offers of amnesty, employment and compensation.

It is possible that the rebellion would have ended without

bloodshed had it not been faced with its own resistance. Within the settlement a small number of men opposed Riel. In mid-February, the group made plans to seize power but was detected before it could act. Forty-eight were apprehended, among them the volatile and eager Thomas Scott. An Orangeman, Scott proved himself a difficult prisoner. He expressed contempt for the Métis, provoked his keepers and uttered death threats against Riel. After two weeks of this behaviour, Scott was tried by an *ad hoc* tribunal, found guilty of treason and was shot by a firing squad.

The execution was a grave miscalculation, one which would ultimately seal Riel's fate. In the greater picture Scott's death poisoned relations between English- and French-speaking Canadians and served to jeopardize negotiations to bring Rupert's Land into Confederation. Unbeknown to Riel, on 3 May, Ottawa had dispatched a force of 1,100 men from Collingwood, Ontario to ensure the transition of government. It was during their arduous journey of 115 days that the Manitoba Act was passed. On 12 May, the territory became the fifth province in the

Dominion; however it was not until 24 August that the expedition arrived at Fort Garry, the seat of the provisional government. It entered the stronghold to find that Riel and the other leaders of the rebellion had fled. Red River, one of the three great rebellions in Canadian history, ended without a single battle.

Riel, having been refused amnesty, settled in the United States; many of his followers left for the newly created Northwest Territories, where they founded a settlement at Batoche on the South Saskatchewan river. However, as settlers from Ontario began to arrive, the Métis again became involved in land disputes.

In May of 1884, they and other discontented settlers resolved to seek Riel's help in presenting their grievances to Ottawa. A delegation headed by Gabriel Dumont met the exiled leader in Montana. Riel required little convincing. During the years following the rebellion, he had come to believe that he was a prophet of the New World, divinely chosen to lead the Métis.

On 19 March 1885, Riel, Dumont and a group composed

mostly of Métis established the 'Provisional Government of Saskatchewan'. In doing so, they began down a path similar to that followed in Manitoba. This time, however, support for Riel was not nearly as strong. The English-speaking settlers of the area were less than sympathetic to Métis aspirations, and the Roman Catholic Church, which had once provided cautious co-operation and counsel, pulled away from this self-proclaimed prophet and his fantastic visions. Indeed, the missionar Father Albert Lacombe obtained assurances from Crowfoot that the Blackfoot would not participate in any rebellion. Not only had Riel failed to rally non-Métis natives, but most of the Métis would withheld support. Where the Red River Rebellion had contained no bloodshed – the execution of Thomas Scott aside – tensions created by the North-West Rebellion quickly became violent.

THE BATTLE *of* FISH CREEK

24 APRIL 1885

————•—•————

THE PROVISIONAL GOVERNMENT of Saskatchewan established by Louis Riel enjoyed only one week of peacetime governance. Yet even in peace there was conflict. Métis rebels had already begun to seize stores and take prisoners. Then, on 26 March 1885, the provisional government was thrown into a war from which it would never emerge.

The catalyst was an attempt by members of the North-West Mounted Police (NWMP) to remove goods and arms from the Duck Lake store before they could be captured by the Métis. However, the rebels, supported by Cree, had already occupied the village. The superintendent of the NWMP, Lief Crozier, endeavoured to parley, but this ended in disaster. A Métis made a grab for the rifle of his interpreter, who in turn drew his revolver, killing two of the rebels. Thus, the fighting of the rebellion began with an image of Crozier running back towards his men while giving the order to open fire.

Holding high his wooden cross, praying aloud, Riel watched from a distance. After less than half an hour, nearly one-third of Crozier's men were casualties, and the superintendent was forced to retreat. Riel considered the victory a sign from God that his government's cause was just.

The Métis may have been victorious at the Battle of Duck Lake, but it was something of a loss for the provisional government. As news of the armed conflict spread, the already shallow support among English-speaking settlers all but evaporated.

The situation for Riel became considerably worse when the Cree chief Wandering Spirit, recognizing the Métis victory, decided to stage an uprising of his own. On 2 April, one week after the Battle of Duck Lake, Wandering Spirit and his warriors forced the non-Native American settlers in the area of Frog Lake to their local church. Nine of his captives were killed, including the local American Indian agent and two Catholic priests.

By this point, Major General Frederick Middleton, General Officer Commanding the Militia of Canada, had arrived in the area. In his 60th year, Middleton had served in India, Malta and at Gibraltar. A well-rounded, intelligent, fun-loving man, his progress up the chain of command in Great Britain had been hindered only by a lack of funds with which to purchase a commission. The young Dominion of Canada offered greater opportunity. 'I have never met a man,' wrote one of Prime Minister Sir John A. Macdonald's correspondents, 'who was less of a "soldier and nothing else" or better able to get on anywhere and with all sorts of people.'

However amiable, Middleton recognized that there could be no negotiation with Riel. From his temporary headquarters at Qu'Appelle, the major general laid out a strategy under which the rebellion would be extinguished and order would be restored. His target was Batoche, approximately 300 km to the north. By striking first at the de-facto seat of the provisional government, Middleton was certain that the flames of rebellion would be quelled.

With a small force, he left Qu'Appelle on 6 April. As the major general made his way toward Batoche, he was joined by troops from the east and two Quebec battalions that had been stationed at Calgary. His force was being assembled when word reached Middleton of the massacre of Frog Lake and the ransacking of the town of Battleford. Middleton had no alternative but to divide his men into three columns. Dispatching two to deal with the new areas of trouble, he continued on to Batoche with a force of slightly more than 800 men. As he drew closer to his destination, Middleton had about half of this force ferried to the opposite shore of the South Saskatchewan, so as to envelop the enemy.

To this point, Gabriel Dumont, Riel's commander-in-chef, had concentrated all efforts on defending Batoche, avoiding any action until the enemy had crossed over into their settlements. However, with the army under Middleton approaching, he felt pressured to go on the attack. His forces set up an ambush at Fish Creek, some 75 km north-east of present-day Saskatoon, and awaited the advancing force in a heavily wooded gully.

Any element of surprise was dashed when approaching militia scouts were fired upon. The gunfire was soon joined by the arrival of the main body of Middleton's column. His men took up positions on the bluffs above Dumont's men. The greater height had no strategic value and, in fact, proved to be something of a hindrance in that it was often impossible to depress guns to a point at which they could fire on Métis positions.

With half his force on the far shore of the South Saskatchewan, Middleton was unable to use his full number to his advantage. Several hours passed before the reinforcements were able to cross over. They arrived just as the weather was turning from a cold drizzle to sleet. Middleton chose not to renew his attack, preferring to withdraw from battle.

At the end of a battle lasting more than six hours, ten members of Middleton's North-West Field Force lay dead; the Métis lost four men.

The major general made no attempt to conceal his disappointment in his men, and yet did not blame them for the defeat. It was clear to Middleton that they simply lacked proper training.

Dumont walked away from the battle recognizing that his force of 200 had triumphed over 900 men. However, his victory was tempered by the knowledge that his men had been running low on provisions and ammunition. It was his luck that Middleton had opted to retreat; it would be his misfortune that the major general would later show less caution.

THE BATTLE *of* CUT KNIFE
2 MAY 1885

———•———

THE GREAT CREE chief Poundmaker played no role in the early days of the rebellion. He had had no involvement in Louis Riel's return from exile, and had no counsel with the Métis leader. And yet Poundmaker handed those fighting for the Canadian government the greatest defeat to have occurred during the rebellion.

The son of a Stony father and mother of mixed blood, Poundmaker was once thought by Ottawa to be among the unlikeliest Native American leaders to cause trouble. In 1876 he had signed Treaty 6, which among other things had guaranteed governmental support in times of pestilence or famine. Five years later, Poundmaker had been selected to accompany the Marquess of Lorne, Governor General of Canada, on a 160-km trip from Battleford to Blackfoot Crossing. A peacemaker, the chief appeared resigned to a less glorious future for his people. Speaking at a feast, he once told them: 'The whites will fill the country, and they will dictate to us as they please. It is useless to dream that we can frighten them; that time has passed. Our only resource is our work, our industry, our farms.'

In 1883, however, Poundmaker moved position to join the discontented. At the root was an austerity programme undertaken by Ottawa that had led to cuts in the Indian Department. Rations were reduced, often arrived late and, it was rumoured, would soon come to an end. During the following winter an unknown number of Native Americans suffered from starvation and malnutrition, yet Ottawa did nothing to change its course. Altercations between the NWMP and the Cree became increasingly frequent.

In the days following the Battle of Duck Lake, Poundmaker set out with a number of Cree and Assiniboine for Battleford, where they intended to discuss their deteriorating situation with the local Indian agent, a man named Rae. Within Battleford, news of the Métis victory at Duck Lake was soon joined by reports that a large number of Native Americans were approaching town. Fearing the unknown, the settlers abandoned their homes for the protection offered by Fort Battleford, the local NWMP barracks. Poundmaker and his party entered an empty town, only to find that Rae refused to leave the fort to meet with them.

For two days, Poundmaker held out the hope that Rae would change his mind. Hungry and frustrated, several of his followers turned to ransacking the town, an act he was unable to halt. On the third day, Poundmaker led his party back to his reserve at Cut Knife Creek.

At Fort Battleford, the small detachment of NWMP called on the General Officer Commanding the Militia of Canada, Major General Frederick Middleton, for reinforcements. He responded by sending a column of 763 men under the leadership of Lieutenant Colonel William Otter. It was anything but a speedy deployment. The column first travelled by rail to Swift Current, from where they set off on a 300-km march north. This last leg of the journey alone took 11 days. When they arrived in Battleford on 24 April, the column found several hundred settlers, including some Métis, still living in the fort.

The relief brought by the arrival of Otter and his men soon led to calls for revenge. After spending six days in the now secure town, Otter and 325 of his men advanced on the reserve at Cut Lake Creek. It was Otter's plan to arrive in the early morning hours, under cover of darkness, and attack while Poundmaker's people were asleep. Ultimately, the strategy was thwarted by the foresight of the Cree chief. Poundmaker was all too aware of the several hundred troops that had moved into the area and had made preparations. After consultations with his war chief, Fine Day, he had the entire encampment – approximately 1,500 men, women and children – moved to the west side of Cut Knife Creek.

By relocating, Poundmaker had forced Otter and his men to ford the creek and wade through a marsh before meeting their enemy. By this point, many hours had passed since the troops had been spotted by Jacob, a Cree elder, who had alerted the camp.

It was well after dawn before Otter was able to determine Poundmaker's new location. He began by directing fire from two antiquated field guns at the camp. The first minutes were ones of complete confusion, as women and children fled for safety. However, the barrage was short-lived; the cannons, having outlived their usefulness, simply fell apart. A Gatling gun proved to be even less effective.

With far fewer resources, Fine Day quickly assumed the upper hand. Having divided his men into groups of four and five, he used a hand mirror with which to signal staggered assaults. As a result, Otter was unable to properly determine his enemy's location, nor could he know from which direction the next attack would occur. What is more, Fine Day's method of attack lent the impression that his force was much larger than it was in actuality.

As the battle entered its seventh hour, Otter ordered a retreat. However, as his soldiers attempted to make their way back across the marsh, the Cree and Assiniboine started a mounted pursuit. It was only through Poundmaker's intervention that a massacre was prevented.

Eight of Otter's soldiers were killed in the Battle of Cut Knife. Poundmaker lost five men, one of whom was a Nez Perce.

Despite the great victory at the Battle of Cut Knife, Poundmaker's authority over the Plains Cree, which had for some years been descendant, continued to fail. He was pressured by Stony warriors to join Riel at Batoche. Now part of the rebellion, he again saved lives by ensuring that members of a captured wagon train were protected and cared for.

On 26 May, after the failure of the resistance became apparent, Poundmaker surrendered to Middleton at Battleford. Two months later, he was tried for treason in Regina. In court, he protested his innocence: 'Everything I could do was done to stop bloodshed. Had I wanted war, I would not be here now. I should be on the prairie. You did not catch me. I gave myself up. You have got me because I wanted justice.'

He served several months in Manitoba's Stony Mountain Penitentiary, before being released a broken man. Four months later, he was dead.

THE BATTLE *of* BATOCHE

9–12 MAY 1885

MAJOR GENERAL Middleton recovered quickly from his defeat at the Battle of Fish Creek, a process which was eased by the arrival on 5 May of the *Northcote*. A modest steamer, it carried a field hospital and much-appreciated provisions.

Reinvigorated, four days later Middleton put into play a new plan of attack on Louis Riel's rebels at Batoche. The strategy involved an attack on two fronts; the main contingent was to advance directly against Métis lines, while along the South Saskatchewan river the *Northcote* would steam past the distracted defenders and disembark 50 men at the rear of the town. However, the terrain proved difficult, and Middleton's ground force soon fell behind schedule. With no artillery fire to contend with, Métis attention was focused entirely on the approaching steamer. Their small arms had little effect on the armoured ship, nevertheless Riel's men managed to inflict considerable damage through the use of a ferry cable. The *Northcote* lost its mast and funnels; crippled, it drifted downriver, away from the battle.

Unaware of the steamer's fate, Middleton approached Mission Ridge, just outside of the town. It was there that his men positioned the artillery and began shelling the settlement. Unfortunately for Middleton, this barrage did not produce the intended result; rather, the brief pause in the advance provided extra time for the Métis to become entrenched.

Recognizing the enemy position, advances by Middleton's men were conducted with caution. Casualties were few.

Faced with this careful approach, the Métis were unable to make any gains. An attempt to capture cannons only resulted in their withdrawal under cover of a Gatling gun. A bold attempt to surround the government troops also met with failure after brushfires intended to screen would not spread. At the day's end, the positions of the government forces and the Métis were little different than when the battle had begun.

In the morning, Middleton's men resumed their shelling of Batoche. The Métis took a more defensive stance, turning back all advances attempted by the government troops. By nightfall, no progress had been made by either side.

On 11 May, Middleton made his first breakthrough. Dispatching a party along the Métis flank while at the same time conducting an advance along the front, he laid bare the enemy's weakness. Dumont simply lacked the manpower both to guard their flank and oppose the frontal assault. For the first time since the battle had begun three days earlier, the government troops gained ground.

The following morning, Middleton put into action a plan which would, he was convinced, bring about Dumont's defeat. The major general would lead a group of mounted troops in a feigned attack on the enemy's flank. Once the Métis had responded, a cannon would sound, signalling his infantry to attack. All went according to plan until the sound of the cannon went unheard. Middleton returned to the government troops' position, where, in a rage, he took his lunch.

The major general might have been in a better mood had he known just how close he was to victory. Exhausted, wounded and weak, the Métis teetered on the brink of defeat. Short of ammunition, some of Dumont's men had been using what little gunpowder remained to fire stones and nails from their rifles.

Middleton was just sitting down to lunch when government troops began an assault on the enemy's left flank and the resistance crumbled. Within minutes the North-West Field Force had advanced down the ridge, driving the Métis from Batoche.

Middleton's victory at the Battle of Batoche brought the North-West Rebellion to an end. Although there were two further battles – the Battle of Frenchman's Butte and the Battle of Loon Lake – they were of no consequence. The greatest significance of the latter rests in the fact that it was the last battle to have been fought on Canadian soil. By 3 June 1885, the day on which it was fought, most of the Provisional Government of Saskatchewan had long fled across the border into the United States. Louis Riel remained in Canada. On 15 May, he was discovered by two scouts and surrendered.

The charges against Riel – indeed, the entire trial process – was influenced significantly by Ontario's Orange Order, who sought justice for the death of Thomas Scott. The disagreeable figure, whose execution had been ordered during the Red River Rebellion, had been mythologized and romanticized. An 1885 novel, *The Story of Louis Riel, the Rebel Chief* by the Newfoundland poet Joseph Edmund Collins, had portrayed a jilted Riel as having ordered Scott's execution as part of a romantic triangle involving a beautiful Métis woman. Though the author later wrote that the story had 'no historic truth', the fantasy was often printed as fact.

Two months after his capture, in *The Queen* versus *Louis Riel*, the Métis leader was tried on six counts of treason. Against his wishes, Riel's legal counsel came to focus on questions of sanity, a defence supported by two doctors and a number of Catholic priests. Riel received a sentence of death and was hanged on 16 November 1885 in Regina.

The North-West Rebellion was the last of the three great rebellions in Canadian history. Lasting just 47 days, it caused more damage than any other, leaving scars that linger still. Although he continued to hold power until the day he died, the execution of Riel proved to be Sir John A. Macdonald's greatest and gravest mistake. The death served to inflame religious and linguistic tensions, and left Macdonald's Conservative party burned.

From the opposition benches, Wilfrid Laurier, who would become one of Macdonald's successors, expressed a rage shared by many Canadians:

Blood! Blood! Blood! Prisons, scaffolds, widows, orphans, destitution, ruin. These are what fill the blank in the administration of this Government of the affairs of the North-West.

In the 1887 election that followed, the opposition Liberals doubled their Quebec representation, while Macdonald's Conservative government lost 19 of its 50 seats in the province. For the next 70 years, the Grits would win the majority of seats in each federal election – 17 in total.

CHAPTER VIII

—•◆•—

The First World War

THE WAR *to* END ALL WARS
1914–18

An introduction

WITH CONFEDERATION in 1868 Canada assumed responsibility for its land defence. In the event of a serious emergency, however, it was understood that Britain would come to the young country's aid. It had done just that during the Red River Rebellion by sending British regulars in support of Canadian militia.

This arrangement was not strictly one-sided. In 1884 and 1885, nearly 400 Canadian volunteers, the Nile Voyageurs, arrived in the Sudan to aid the British in their evacuation of the country.

Fifteen years later, Canada was asked to contribute to the

United Kingdom's struggle with the Orange Free State and the South African Republic in the Second Boer War. This business of the empire brought crisis to the government of Sir Wilfrid Laurier and split his Liberal Party along pro- and anti-imperialist lines. A fairly fragile compromise was negotiated in which a force of approximately 7,400 Canadian volunteers was sent in aid of the British cause. Two hundred and twenty-four died and 252 were wounded in the fighting.

Greater sacrifice was to come.

On 4 August 1914, the United Kingdom entered the First World War. As Canada still held colonial status, it was automatically drawn in through the mother country's declaration of war on Germany. However, while the Canadian government had had no say in entering the war, it was permitted to decide its level of involvement.

In all, Canada sent four divisions overseas to fight in Europe. Then a nation of 8,000,000, a total of 619,636 citizens served. Roughly one in nine – 66,655 – were killed, with another 172,950 wounded.

With Canadian participation, particularly in the battles of Ypres, Vimy Ridge and Passchendaele and Amiens, the country earned a greater place on the world stage. Canada, which in 1914 had had no say in the declaration of war on Germany, sent its own delegates to negotiate the Treaty of Versailles.

Even before it began, the First World War was being called 'The Great War'. As it dragged on, another description was given: 'The War to End All Wars'. This hope is evident in a 3 July 1921 speech by Arthur Meighen, the first Canadian prime minister to visit Vimy Ridge. At Thelus Military Cemetery he delivered an address entitled 'The Glorious Dead':

> *The Great War is past; the war that tried through and through every quality and mystery of the human spirit; the war that closed, we hope for ever, the long, ghastly story of the arbitrament of men's differences by force; the last clash and crash of earth's millions is over now ... We live among the ruins and the echoes of Armageddon.*

Its shadow is receding slowly backward into history.

At this time the proper occupation of the living is, first, to honour our heroic dead; next, to repair the havoc, human and material, that surrounds us; and, lastly, to learn aright and apply with courage the lessons of the war.

THE SECOND BATTLE *of* YPRES

22 APRIL–25 MAY 1915

——•——

AT THE TIME of the First Battle of Ypres, fought over a 34-day period in the autumn of 1914, the bulk of the soldiers in the Canadian Expeditionary Force were training on England's Salisbury Plain. There they spent several miserable months of preparation under cold drizzle and sleet in the shadow, when there was sun to cast one, of Stonehenge. Though the conditions were miserable, they were nothing compared to the horrors experienced by the armies of the United Kingdom, France and the German Empire fighting at Ypres. All told, casualties in the First Battle of Ypres reached 238,000, the majority of whom were Germans. During the battle, eight units of the German Empire made up of enthusiastic young volunteers had been met by a British force of experienced veterans of the Second Boer War. The horrific consequence was reflected within the German Empire, where the battle became known as *Kindermord zu Ypren* – the Massacre of the Innocents at Ypres.

The First Battle of Ypres marked the conclusion of the German movement towards the North Sea. In its wake, this 'Race to the Sea' left more than 800 km of trenches, bringing an end to mobile warfare on the Western Front. As a result, in February 1915, when the 1st Canadian Division arrived on continental Europe, they received training in trench warfare from experienced British soldiers.

After two months holding a line in the relatively quiet Armentières sector in French Flanders, the Canadians joined the Allied forces at the Ypres Salient. The northernmost portion of the salient was held by two French divisions; the Canadians took position at the centre, with two divisions from the United Kingdom to their right.

In the late afternoon of 22 April, the Germans released 168 tons (152 tonnes) of chlorine gas over a 6-km stretch of the salient held by the French troops. Although the Germans had deployed poison gas three months earlier during the Battle of Bolimov on the Eastern Front, the gas employed – xylyl bromide – proved greatly ineffective. The use of chlorine at the Ypres Salient caught the allies entirely unprepared. Within ten minutes, 6,000 French, Algerian and Moroccan troops lay dead, primarily from asphyxiation. Others were killed when, seeking to escape the heavy gas filling their trenches, they scrambled out into enemy fire. Those who survived did so by abandoning their positions – some fleeing towards Ypres, others hoping for safety in the Canadian trenches – opening a large gap in the front line.

The effectiveness of the gas far exceeded expectations. The German command had conceived of no major breakthrough and had brought in no reserves. Wearing primitive respirators, two of their corps advanced with caution and hesitation. As dusk descended, the Canadians moved in to re-establish a continuous, if fragile, line. Several hours later, as midnight approached, members of the Calgary Highlanders and the Canadian Scottish Regiment launched a counter-attack in which they managed to drive the Germans from the neighbouring dense wood of Bois-de-Cuisinères. Two other assaults, though less successful, managed to purchase time, allowing for strengthening of what was once the French position.

On the morning of 24 April, the original Canadian position to the west of the village of Saint-Julien came under violent bombardment. This was followed by another chlorine gas attack, which was accompanied by machine-gun fire. Despite the approaching green-yellow cloud, the Canadians were able to fight on through the use of handkerchiefs they had soaked in their own urine. A quick-thinking soldier recognized that when placed over the nose and mouth, the urea within the urine reacted with the chlorine, effectively neutralizing it.

Fighting under these less than idyllic conditions, Saint-Julien was lost to the Germans. After 48 hours of fighting, the first significant combat experienced by the 1st Canadian Division, casualties amounted to one in three of their number – more than 2,000 lay dead with a further 4,000 injured.

Over the next two days, the Canadians received some relief from the British who attempted to take back Saint-Julien.

Though they failed in this objective, a new line just outside the village was established. The general in charge of the assault, Horace Lockwood Smith-Dorien, soon determined that nothing but a massive counter-offensive would have any chance of success. Smith-Dorien's recommendation that the Allied forces withdraw 3 km led immediately to his dismissal. However, his replacement, General Herbert Plumer, proposed the very same strategy. Between 1 and 3 May, the planned withdrawal was executed. Five days later, within the vicinity of Ypres, fighting was renewed when the Germans attempted to break Allied lines. On 10 May, the surgeon and poet Major John McCrae wrote to his mother:

I have done what fell to hand. My clothes, boots, kit, and dugout at various times were sadly bloody. Two of our batteries are reduced to two officers each. We have had constant accurate shell-fire, but we have given back no less. And behind it all was the constant background of the sights of the dead, the wounded, the maimed, and a terrible anxiety lest the line should give way.

That same day and on 24 May, chlorine gas was again used, but to lesser effect than previously. Although the Germans managed to make some gains, these came at great cost. It is likely that the strategy of Smith-Dorien and Plumer prevented the destruction of the Ypres Salient.

Lacking both supplies and manpower, the Germans finally ended their offensive on 25 May and turned their attention on Ypres itself. Shelling reduced the damaged city to rubble.

Although territory had been lost, the Allies had frustrated German attempts at breaking their line. The cost had been great; casualties on the Allied side amounted to nearly 70,000, twice that suffered by the Germans.

The Ypres Salient had been reduced to a depth of 5 km.

The use of chlorine at the Second Battle of Ypres proved the climax in what had been an escalating chemical war. The first combatants to resort to gas warfare were not the Germans, as is commonly believed, but the French. In August of 1914, they had fired tear-gas grenades at German lines. Two months later, the Germans fired shells containing a chemical irritant at the French. The subsequent effect, a fit of sneezing, verged on the comical, and stood in stark contrast to the horrors at Ypres. When combined with water, such as that found within the body, chlorine gas forms hydrochloric acid which destroys moist tissues.

Contributing to the tragedy at Ypres is the fact that captured German troops had revealed its impending use.

The employment of chlorine gas by the Germans brought immediate condemnation and damaged its relations with the United States and other then-neutral countries. The German Empire attempted some limited repair work through a statement issued on 25 June 1915, in which it asserted that the French had pioneered the use of asphyxiating gases in the months leading to the Second Battle of Ypres.

Ultimately, the German use of chlorine gas dispelled any hesitancy on behalf of the Allied powers. On the morning of 25 September 1915, the United Kingdom would launch the Battle of Loos by releasing more than 400 tons (363 tonnes) of chlorine gas.

Following the Second Battle of Ypres, both sides worked unceasingly towards more sophisticated chemical weapons and protective-wear. After April 1915, the use of gas would not come as a surprise, and as a result, would never again be particularly effective.

More than any other conflict, the First World War is known for the verse that it inspired and the poets that it killed. The battlefield at Ypres claimed Colwyn Philipps, R.W. Sterling, Francis Ledwidge, W.S.S. Lyon and Julian Grenfell, whose 'Into Battle' had served to inspire British and Canadian soldiers in the early years. It was, however, the death of a soldier who was not a poet which would have the greatest impact in the field of letters. On the morning of 2 May, Lieutenant Alexis Helmer, an officer in the 2nd Battery, 1st Brigade Canadian Field Artillery, was struck by a German shell. His body parts, those that could be found, were gathered in saddlebags and buried in a simple service conducted by his friend Major John McCrae. It was after this ritual that McCrae composed

what has been described as the war's most popular poem,
'In Flanders Fields':

> *In Flanders fields the poppies blow*
> *Between the crosses, row on row,*
> *That mark our place; and in the sky*
> *The larks, still bravely singing, fly*
> *Scarce heard amid the guns below.*
> *We are the Dead. Short days ago*
> *We lived, felt dawn, saw sunset glow,*
> *Loved and were loved, and now we lie*
> *In Flanders fields.*
>
> *Take up our quarrel with the foe:*
> *To you from failing hands we throw*
> *The torch; be yours to hold it high.*
> *If ye break faith with us who die*
> *We shall not sleep, though poppies grow*
> *In Flanders fields.*

THE BATTLE *of* THE SOMME

1 JULY–18 NOVEMBER 1916

———•———

THE SUMMER SOLSTICE of 1916 marked the start of the seventh season since the trenches had put an end to mobile warfare on the Western Front. Neither the Allies nor the German Empire had proved capable of resolving the stalemate. The former had concluded that no tactical innovation or new technology would provide a solution – it was brute force that was required.

This new Allied strategy, decided upon the previous December, centred on simultaneous mid-year assaults on the three fronts. On the Western Front, a joint British and French offensive was to take place along the front to the north and south of the River Somme. The planning had only just begun when, on 21 February, the strategy was upset by a German attack on the city and commune of Verdun-sur-Meuse. The resulting Battle of Verdun consumed much of the French war effort for the balance of the year. In fact, fighting continued until 18 December, a total of more than 300 days. As Christmas approached and peace settled into the region, the dead were recorded as 303,000, more than half of whom were French.

Beginning early in the nightmarish battle, the French pressured Britain's new commander-in-chief, Field Marshal Sir Douglas Haig, to rush the Somme offensive in order to relieve pressure in Verdun. What had once been intended as a joint offensive now fell almost entirely to the British Empire.

Though French participation had had to be reduced, Haig managed an enormous build-up of men and arms. He became convinced that the German lines would be destroyed, allowing the cavalry into the open countryside, where it could attack battery positions and disrupt communications.

However, the German army, long forewarned of the attack and able to discern at least some of the Allies' preparation, had engaged in a massive restructuring of their defences, most especially in the northern area of the British attack. They were firmly entrenched along the ridges and the villages of the northern Somme countryside.

One British preparation, of which the Germans were unaware, was the excavation of 17 tunnels through which mines were planted.

Beginning on 25 June, the Germans suffered an intense bombardment, during which British artillery fired more than 1,700,000 shells. Five days later, on the morning of 1 July, the enemy experienced explosions of a different sort when mines placed beneath their front-line trenches were fired.

Two minutes later, a 40-km front consisting of several thousand French and British troops, and including units from Newfoundland and Bermuda, began an advance across No Man's Land, resulting in one of the greatest slaughters in military history. More than 57,000 British soldiers were killed, wounded or went missing – a number which continues as the heaviest losses ever suffered by the British army in a single day. Included in the British number were 733 of the 801-member 1st Battalion of the Newfoundland Regiment – cut down within an hour's exposure outside the commune of Beaumont-Hamel. Every one of their officers was listed among the dead or wounded.

Within the carnage lay a very small measure of success; for the most part, the French had achieved their objectives, while Britain's divisions in the south had also gained ground. The rest however, more than two-thirds of the British sector, had precious little to show for its immense loss.

Throughout the summer months, fighting continued – nearly always with no significant gain. Any small measure of success stood out from the dismal failure of Haig's plan. Still the fighting continued, though the field marshal himself had come to recognize that the possibility of success was remote at best.

In late August 1916, under the command of Lieutenant General Julian Byng, the newly formed Canadians Corps were moved from the Ypres Salient to join the front line at the Somme. They took over a section just west of the German-held village of Courcelette, but encountered heavy combat before they could launch a full-scale assault. The corps' number was reduced by more than 2,600 casualties before their first offensive.

On 15 September, the Canadians joined with the British

for an assault along a 2-km stretch of the front close to their own lines. Here there was something of a breakthrough, an accomplishment due to the debut of the tank. Though unreliable, vulnerable and capable of a speed of little more than 3 km/h, the appearance of several of the 'new engines of war' intimidated the Germans, and helped greatly in pushing back their line.

Over the course of just a few hours Canadian and British troops advanced, taking and holding Courcelette. However, as the tanks began to get bogged down and their frailties were revealed, progress slowed. Fighting intensified with the arrival the next day of German reinforcements. From this point on, any movement by either side was insignificant; the stagnation brought by trench warfare had once again taken hold.

The Allies' final accomplishment of any note occurred on 26 September when the Canadians managed to push the German line a further kilometre away from Courcelette.

Again and again the Canadian Corps attacked German entrenchments, with frustrating results. More than a month was consumed in an attempt to take and hold the Regina

Trench. Thought to be central to German defences, it was revealed as little more than a depression when finally taken on 11 November.

One week later, the battle ended. Advances came to an end as the cold heavy rains of autumn reduced the battlefield to mud, rendering further offensives pointless.

Four and a half months had elapsed since the battle had started. In that time the Allies had managed to advance their line by as much as 8 km. The territory had been gained at a cost of nearly 630,000 men, more than 146,000 of whom had been killed. The Germans, who came to refer to the Battle of the Somme as *das Blutbad* – The Blood Bath – suffered 164,055 killed and 270,460 wounded.

The Canadians, who had been at the Somme for three months, lost 24,029 men. Their reputation as a fearless fighting force, established in confronting the clouds of chlorine gas at the Second Battle of Ypres, was solidified and recognized on both sides of the trenches. In his candid *War Memoirs of David Lloyd George*, the British prime minister of the Great War writes of the Battle of the Somme:

The Canadians played a part of such distinction that thenceforward they were marked out as storm troops; for the remainder of the war they were brought along to head the assault in one great battle after another. Whenever the Germans found the Canadian Corps coming into the line they prepared for the worst.

THE BATTLE *of* VIMY RIDGE
9–12 APRIL 1917

————•————

A 'DEFINING MOMENT', 'the birth of a nation' – of all that has been written in the nine decades that have followed, it is perhaps historian Desmond Morton who has described it best: 'For Canadians, Vimy Ridge was a nation-building experience. For some, then and later, it symbolized the fact that the Great War was also Canada's war of independence.'

It is often considered the moment at which the Dominion shed its colonial cloak and took its place on the world stage.

Approximately 7 km in length with an elevation of just less than 150 m, Vimy Ridge afforded a commanding view of both German-held territory and the Allied lines. It had been taken by the Germans during the First Battle of Artois in early October 1914, little more than two months after the war had begun. The following May, during the Second Battle of Artois, the French had managed to briefly take back the ridge, but soon lost it due to a lack of reinforcements. This effort and others, including the Third Battle of Artois, had cost the French more than 150,000 casualties. The German Sixth Army had since fortified the ridge with artillery, machine-gun nests, barbed wire and three rows of trenches. Beneath it all was a maze of tunnels that had been built by tunnelling companies through porous, yet stable, chalk.

Relative quiet had followed the Third Battle of Artois; this was broken rather abruptly when, in February 1916, the British took over the sector, relieving the French. The tunnels were discovered, the Royal Engineer Tunnelling Companies were deployed and soon underground clashes brought death to soldiers of both sides – a great many were buried alive.

Responding to the broken calm in early May 1916, the German Empire pounded British positions with heavy artillery and mortar fire. This was followed by a successful assault by the German infantry in which British mine craters were captured.

By October of 1916, Allied casualties incurred through

efforts to seize the ridge had risen to 300,000. That same month a new military unit, the Canadian Corps, relieved the British stationed along the western slopes of the ridge. The corps had been formed just one month after the arrival in France of the 2nd Canadian Division. Initially commanded by Lieutenant Colonel Sir Edwin Alfred Hervey Alderson, his position came to be filled by Field Marshal Julian Byng, a much more effective and popular leader who would one day be installed as the twelfth Governor General of Canada. The field marshal knew Vimy well. In fact, it had been Byng who, as commander of the British XVII Corps, had discovered the existence of German mining the previous February.

As winter set in formal discussions began among corps commanders, Byng included, about a spring offensive near Arras, 8 km south-west of Vimy Ridge. As the months passed and work on strategy progressed, the Canadian Corps objective became clear; it would not participate at Arras, rather it would attack Vimy Ridge. Diversionary in purpose, the assault was intended to allow the southern flank of the Arras offensive to advance without being fired upon by the Germans along the ridge.

For the first time, all four divisions of the Canadian Corps – a total of 97,184 men – would be together in combat. They would be joined by the British 5th Infantry Division, and several engineer and labour units.

In preparation, British tunnelling crews aided the Canadians in expanding the vast underground networks and fortifications already in existence. Twelve passages, each more than 1 km in length, connected the reserve lines to front lines, thus allowing the Canadians to advance without being seen. Other areas were hollowed out to create command posts, communication centres, ammunition stores and small hospitals. Still more tunnels were created for the sole purpose of laying mines under German positions.

Planning for the assault on Vimy Ridge rested on Byng and Major General Arthur Currie, a veteran of the Second Battle of Ypres. Currie recommended that they adopt a French practice of distributing detailed maps to all involved in the battle – a privilege previously afforded only to officers.

Platoon-level training was implemented until each member was capable of carrying out any and all responsibilities. The roles of infantrymen were made more flexible through additional training as riflemen, machine-gunners and grenade-throwers. Sections of the ridge were replicated for rehearsal. Finally, all were trained to advance under what came to be known as a 'creeping barrage'. Credited to Currie, this innovation called for troops to follow advancing lines of shellfire – violence which would also serve to shield the Canadians. This movement added much gravity to the planning, as reflected in a warning issued by Byng: 'Chaps, you shall go over exactly like a railroad train, on time, or you shall be annihilated'.

The Canadian Corps trained for four months. From their vantage point on Vimy Ridge, the German forces could not help but notice the preparations and recognized that a major attack was imminent.

On 25 March 1917, shells began raining down on the Germans, beginning a period they would come to call 'The Week of Suffering'. Each and every hour, over the course of the next seven days, the barrage continued. More than a million shells fell on German trenches.

At dawn on 9 April, a particularly cold, rain-drenched Easter Monday, the Canadian Corps began the attack on Vimy Ridge. The mines that had been laid beneath the German position were fired and assault divisions advanced along a front of more than 6 km, under cover of the creeping barrage. The first wave numbered 15,000 Canadians, the first of nearly 100,000 hoping to take and hold the ridge. At their backs were more than 1,000 cannons, including heavy artillery mounted on railway cars several kilometres from the battlefield.

In less than two hours, the corps captured three of their four objectives. All had gone according to schedule, with only one exception: Hill 145. The highest point of the ridge, it received less damage from the Allied barrage. As a result, the Germans were able to fire upon the advancing Canadians of the 4th Division with considerable effect. In just six minutes, more than 60 per cent of the assaulting company were shot to death. Despite the great loss, by day's end the Canadians managed to seize the hill.

With the coming of light the following morning, the 4th Division moved east of Hill 145 in an assault on still-active German trenches.

On 12 April, amid a blinding snowstorm, the last of the German resistance ended; the Canadians Corps controlled the entire 7-km ridge.

For Canada, the cost was greater than any battle before or since: 3,598 had been killed; a further 7,004 were wounded.

The poet Canon F.G. Scott, head chaplain of the 1st Canadian Division, reflected on the losses: 'In spite of the numbers of wounded and dying men which I had seen, the victory was such a complete and splendid one that April 9th, 1917, was one of the happiest days in my life.'

The German Sixth Army suffered more than 20,000 casualties, a massive number that would, in the Second World War, be overshadowed by their losses at the Battle of Stalingrad.

Reduced by their dead, their wounded and the loss of a further 4,000 who became prisoners of war, the Sixth Army retreated downwards to the Plains of Douai. As they had believed Vimy Ridge to have been entirely impregnable, German morale was terribly undermined.

The victory at Vimy Ridge had a different effect in Canada. It marked the first time in the young nation's 50-year history that a corps-sized formation fought as a unit. Despite the casualties, the assault was considered an overwhelming success, and provided a lift to the Allies at a time when the disaster of the Somme still felt fresh.

After the victory at Vimy, Julian Byng was given command of the British Third Army. He was later raised to the peerage as 1st Baron Byng of Vimy and Thorpe-le-Soken.

Arthur Currie received a knighthood from George V on the battlefield. He took over command of the Canadian Corps, the first from the Dominion to be so honoured.

The accomplishment by the Canadian Corps at Vimy was recognized by the French government who, in 1922, ceded the ridge to the people of Canada. The tunnels, trenches and craters of the Great War remain to this day, now towered over by the white limestone Canadian National Vimy Memorial. Canada's largest, the war monument took 11 years to build at a cost of more than $1,500,000. It stands on the highest point of the ridge, Hill 145, the spot that had once been covered by German machine-gun nests.

The Battle *of* Passchendaele

31 July–6 November 1917

I<small>F</small>, AS SOME attest, the Battle of Vimy Ridge gave birth to a nation, the Battle of Passchendaele reminded Canadians that they were still very much a colony. The engagement was not one in which they wanted to take part. It was recognized as folly by Lieutenant General Sir Arthur Currie, the newly-installed commander of the Canadian Corps. When called upon to join the battle three months after the fighting had begun, the lieutenant general protested that the time was not right for a Canadian assault. He predicted, with alarming accuracy, that 16,000 members of the Corps would be lost.

Of all the controversies in the First World War, that which surrounded this particular battle was by far the greatest. In a time dominated by propaganda and marked by a hesitancy within English-speaking Canada and the United Kingdom at expressing dissent, the strategy employed was condemned and criticized as vain and reckless. Where the deaths at Vimy Ridge had been considered a glorious sacrifice, the losses in the Battle of Passchendaele were viewed as a contemptible waste of human life.

The clash was yet another attempt by the Allies at breaking the stalemate that had taken root in the trenches of the front line. Three years had passed since the 'Race for the Sea', a time marked by persistent shelling and periodic attempts by the Allies at breaking through the German lines. Their greatest achievement, the success at the Battle of Vimy Ridge, was not exploited. The offensive that it had been intended to support had failed, leading to large losses and, eventually, mutinies within the French forces. Weakened, Brigadier General Henri Philippe Pétain, commander-in-chief of the French army and future leader of Vichy France, was forced to adopt a more defensive role. After May 1917, he conducted few very offensive manoeuvres; those that did take place were extremely limited in scope and intent. Pétain's strategy was to strengthen his army while awaiting the arrival of the once isolationist Americans, who had declared war on Germany the previous month.

The Pétain plan was viewed with disdain by Sir Douglas Haig, the British commander-in-chief. Determined that major offensive engagements should continue, he looked towards the Ypres Salient, which he was convinced would provide the greatest opportunity for a breakthrough. In this belief he was supported by the Royal Navy, which hoped that capturing the ports on the Belgian coast, then being used as bases for German submarines, would eliminate enemy attacks on British seaborne trade. Haig's strategy involved punching a hole in the German lines and the capture of Passchendaele Ridge, to be followed by an advance to the English Channel.

For the Allies, the Battle of Passchendaele was a disaster from the start. Artillery bombardments, designed to eliminate the enemy's defensive trench network, obliterated the region's drainage system. This destruction, in combination with an unusual period of constant rain – forecasts of which Haig ignored – transformed what was largely reclaimed marshland into a sea of mud and stagnant water. Movement was difficult; newly introduced tanks became bogged down and equipment simply disappeared, swallowed up by liquid-like mud. The marshy terrain made the digging of trenches impossible, leaving all engaged in each assault exposed to artillery and machine-gun fire.

Meanwhile, the Germans remained secure and relatively dry, sheltered from the rain and shells in a series of heavily constructed, interlocking pillboxes.

By October the British troops had gained little, though their casualties had been high. In the middle of the month the Canadian Corps joined the front line, taking up position between the British and the Australian and New Zealand Army Corps.

As at Vimy Ridge, Currie had done as much planning as time would permit. He devised a strategy through which Passchendaele would be taken in a series of engagements, each with a narrow objective. Together they would support the overall goal of driving a wedge into the position of the German army.

The Canadian Corps launched their first assault shortly

after dawn on 26 October, with the 3rd and 4th Divisions attempting an advance over a deteriorating field of mud through a cold rain. After three days of fighting, the Canadians had gained 700 m at a cost of more than 2,500 casualties.

The very next day, 30 October, a second assault was launched with similarly devastating consequences. Within 24 hours, the Canadians suffered a further 2,300 dead or wounded – all for no more than another kilometre of ground.

A week later, a third attack was launched. Soldiers of the 1st and 2nd Divisions waded through waist-deep water to liberate the village of Passchendaele, situated on the ridge, some 12 km to the north-east of Ypres.

The fourth and final assault occurred on 10 November, securing the high ground atop Passchendaele Ridge. It was only then, after 98 days of fighting, that Haig ordered an end to the offensive. The decisive victory of which he had been so very confident was well beyond his site.

The fighting over, the Battle of Passchendaele was immediately recognized for what it was: a futile struggle, fought under horrendous conditions. The suffering had been immense: while the Germans incurred approximately 260,000 casualties, more than 448,000 Allied soldiers were dead or wounded. Canadian casualties amounted to 15,654, just a few hundred fewer than Currie had predicted.

Ninety-eight days of battle had produced no gains of any significance. All the territory taken during the battle would be ceded within six months. While some defended the decision to pursue the battle by observing that it had served to wear down the Germans, the Allies were, if anything, more weakened. Images of soldiers drowning in pools of torpid water mixed with blood remained in the public consciousness. Haig was disgraced. Among his critics was Lloyd George, the British prime minister, who wrote that the Battle of Passchendaele 'would count among the greatest, most difficult, most sinister, most futile and bloodiest battles ever fought in the entire history of warfare.'

THE BATTLE *of* AMIENS
8–11 AUGUST 1918

———•———

GERMAN GENERAL Erich Ludendorff characterized 8 August 1918, the beginning of the Battle of Amiens, as the 'Black Day of the German Army'. The first phase of the Hundred Days Offensive – known in France as *Les cent jours du Canada*' – it would ultimately lead to the Allied victory in the First World War.

The Hundred Days Offensive followed *Kaiserschlacht* – the Kaiser's Battle – a German offensive which had begun the previous March with an assault on the right wing of the British Expeditionary Force. Although successful in the early stages, making the greatest advances by either side in more than three years, as the months passed success was mixed with increasing measures of failure. Led by Ludendorff, the final *Kaiserschlacht* assault, the 18 July Second Battle of the Marne, ended in defeat.

As the Germans withdrew, the French and British were

working on plans for an attack to take place at Amiens, a small city and commune situated some 120 km to the north of Paris.

Surprise was considered a key element in the planned offensive. Extensive use would be made of advances in aerial photographic reconnaissance, thus eliminating ranging shots, which had been considered essential in assuring accurate fire. Indeed, there would be no artillery fire whatsoever until just prior to the Allied advance. The troop movement would be preceded by a creeping barrage, first used to such great effect the previous year at the Battle of Vimy Ridge.

The greatest surprise of all would come from four infantry divisions of the Canadian Corps, which had managed to enter Amiens undetected by the enemy. In fact, a feint had led the Germans to believe that the Canadians were all on their way north to Flanders.

Kaiserschlacht had been motivated by two factors: the freeing of nearly 50 divisions after the Russian surrender and recognition that the United States' entry into the war would soon bring an influx of material and troops to the Allied side.

Their offensive having ground to a halt, the Germans expected that they might soon be forced into a defensive position. While they considered four likely targets of an Allied assault, not one of these was Amiens. In fact, the Allies had been ignoring Amiens for the specific purpose of drawing German attention to other areas of the front.

On 6 August, two days before the planned assault at Amiens, the German Second Army attacked north of the Somme River. They gained 700 m on a section of the front upon which the Allies had intended to attack. Although some ground was ceded the following day, the incident occasioned adjustments to the Allied plan.

Just after four o'clock on the foggy morning of 8 August, Canadian, British and Australian forces attacked the front to the north and south of the Somme. After an intentional delay of 45 minutes, they were joined by the French.

Though the use of gas was minimal, fighting was fierce.

It took more than three hours before the first German position was captured.

With armoured support, the Canadian and Australian forces in the centre managed to breach the German line. They advanced at a rapid pace, pushing the line 5 km forwards and capturing German officers as they ate breakfast. Such were the advances made by the Canadians and Australians that the divisions involved outdistanced their supporting artillery.

The 15-km gap that the Canadians and Australians had created could not be closed. Progress was not nearly so great on the north side of the river, where the British had to contend with rougher terrain and the sudden changes in plans forced by the German territorial gains made just two days earlier.

Nevertheless, by the end of the day the Germans had lost more than 30,000 men, 16,000 of whom were captured by Allied forces.

For three more days the Allied assault continued against an enemy suffering increasingly from low morale. Positions were abandoned and by 11 August the Germans had pulled out of the area.

German forces suffered 74,000 casualties at the Battle of Amiens, more than three times the Allies' number. The pride taken in the gains made during the four months of the *Kaiserschlacht* offensive vanished under the significant loss of territory to the Allies. The stalemate brought by the trenches in the autumn of 1914 had been well and truly broken. General Ludendorff's 'Black Day' would be followed by 95 more before the signing of the Armistice on 11 November 1918.

CHAPTER IX

---•---

The Second World War

THE STRUGGLE AGAINST FASCISM
1939–45

An introduction

IF THE 1914–18 conflict was the Great War, that which began two decades later might be considered the Greater War, since the fighting encircled the globe. When Parliament voted its support of the decision to go to war on 10 September 1939, Canada had not yet recovered from a decade-long economic depression. The battles fought under the governments of R.B. Bennett and William Lyon Mackenzie King had been economic.

The country entered the war gradually. While Canada fought in the Battle of Britain and more significantly the Battle of the Atlantic, it wasn't until the Battle of Hong

Kong, in December 1941, that Canadians participated in ground combat.

Of the Second World War battles in which Canadians fought, the invasion of Normandy is the most famous. With the British and Americans, the 3rd Canadian Division, the 2nd Canadian Armoured and Canadian Airborne formed the largest seaborne invasion of all time. A great victory, celebrated by its allies, in Canada it is forever linked in public consciousness with the Dieppe Raid.

It is thought that the population of Canada had just passed 11,000,000 when it declared war on Germany. Ten per cent served in the armed forces. Over 42,000 Canadians were killed in the war; a further 55,000 were wounded.

THE BATTLE *of* HONG KONG
8–25 DECEMBER 1941

IN 1902, THE United Kingdom and Japan became allies, promising neutrality if either became involved in a war and support if the conflict involved more than one power. Driven by opposition to Russian expansionism, the Anglo-Japanese Alliance proved to be mutually beneficial during the First World War. Japan was obliged to join in Britain's struggle against Germany. In doing so, its imperialist ambitions were furthered through the seizure of German possessions in the Pacific.

After the Armistice, the alliance began to fade. Germany and Russia, once threats and rivals, had been neutralized. Japan now had few significant obstacles in the way of its own expansionist aspirations in the Pacific and Far East. The growing warmth in the relationship between the United Kingdom and the United States, with whom Japan had frequently come into conflict, placed further strain on the Anglo-Japanese Alliance.

At the 1921 Imperial Conference held in London, Canadian Prime Minister Arthur Meighen spoke in opposition to the alliance with Japan, arguing that its renewal would only serve to alienate the United States and China. A man known for his eloquence, Meighen managed to sway the other attendees, including the Lord Chancellor of the British Empire. All but dead, two years later the treaty reached its official termination.

Tension between the former allies began to escalate, and became particularly stressed after the July 1937 outbreak of the Second Sino-Japanese War. By this time, the British had already begun construction of new defences at Hong Kong, all intended to confront an attack from Japan. The centrepiece of the defences was Gin Drinker's Line, a string of trenches, machine gun nests, fortified bunkers and artillery batteries in the New Territories on the Chinese mainland.

Construction was complete when, in October 1938,

British interests were threatened further by the Japanese occupation of Guangzhou. Hong Kong was now effectively surrounded.

With the beginning of the Second World War, the Hong Kong garrison charged with protecting the colony was severely reduced. Japan, though still at war with China, had not entered the conflict. Designated an outpost, it was felt that the British and Commonwealth troops normally assigned to Hong Kong could be put to better use elsewhere.

However, as both the Second Sino-Japanese War and Second World War progressed, it was believed that military deterrents might be needed to confront Japanese aggression. Approximately 13,000 troops of the British and British Indian armies were sent to the colony, where they came under the command of Major General C. M. Maltby. At the request of Britain, on 16 November 1941, two Canadian infantry battalions – Quebec's Royal Rifles of Canada and Manitoba's Winnipeg Grenadiers – arrived from Vancouver to reinforce the Hong Kong garrison. They were Quebec's Royal Rifles of Canada and Manitoba's

Winnipeg Grenadiers. Prior to being sent to Hong Kong, the Royal Rifles had been posted in Newfoundland and New Brunswick, while the Grenadiers had served in Jamaica.

Both were fairly inexperienced forces, composed mainly of those whose military training was limited; and yet it was these 1,975 soldiers who would become the first Canadian ground units to see action in the Second World War.

The Royal Rifles and Grenadiers had been in Hong Kong just 38 days when, on the morning of 8 December 1941, Japanese bombers began pounding the British planes on the ground at Kai Tak Airport.

Arriving just seven hours after the attack on Pearl Harbor, the sudden appearance of the Japanese aircraft had come as no surprise, however. Indeed, the entire garrison had already been ordered to war stations. The Canadians had taken up position at Wong Nei Chong Gap in the centre of Hong Kong Island.

The bombers were followed by Japanese ground forces advancing from the Chinese mainland. Moving across the frontier of the New Territories, they easily overcame resistance from the Commonwealth's advance units. Although the forward forces had to retreat to the Gin Drinkers' Line, they hoped to defend against the Japanese for at least a week. However, this 'Oriental Maginot Line' proved, if anything, even less effective than its namesake. On the second day of battle, the Japanese ground forces captured Shing Mun Redoubt, the single most important strategic position on the line's left flank. This victory provided just one indication of how much Maltby had underestimated the enemy. Launched under cover of darkness, the assault followed a dispatch in which the major general had observed that 'Japanese night work was poor'.

On 10 December, the Winnipeg Grenadiers' 'D' Company was sent to reinforce the defence of the mainland. The following day, they became the first Canadian army unit to engage in combat in the Second World War. Within hours of this event, Maltby ordered the abandonment of the Gin Drinker's Line. All Commonwealth troops on the mainland evacuated to Hong Kong Island. Once there, the forces were divided into East and West brigades. The

East Brigade, led by British Brigadier Cedric Wallis, was composed of the Royal Rifles of Canada, together with soldiers from the British Indian Army. The Winnipeg Grenadiers, with British and British Indian troops formed the West Brigade under Brigadier J.K. Lawson.

The mainland having been won, the Japanese directed their attention at weakening the island through air raids, artillery bombardment and the targeting of pillboxes spread across the north shore. They twice demanded that Hong Kong be surrendered, and were both times met with rejection from Sir Mark Aitchison Young, governor of the colony.

There was no chance of rescue, yet, as late as 18 December, some in command expressed the belief that there would be no Japanese attempt to take Hong Kong Island. This was put to lie the very same evening when the Japanese launched four separate amphibious assaults across a 3-km stretch of the island's north-east beaches. Once ashore they were confronted by the machine-gun fire of the British Indian Rajput Battalion emanating from the pillboxes. The

Royal Rifles engaged the enemy, attempting to push them back to the shore. Fierce fighting continued throughout the night, leading to heavy casualties on both sides.

Despite the very best efforts of the Commonwealth forces, they were overwhelmed by the sheer number of the invading force.

By early the next morning, the Japanese had destroyed the headquarters of the West Brigade and had reached the Wong Nei Chong and Tai Tam gaps. The Rajput Battalion had been all but exterminated in its attempt to defend the island, leaving the East Brigade severely reduced in strength.

During the second full day of fighting, the Japanese succeeded in dividing the island in two.

For five more days, the East and West brigades engaged in a hopeless struggle to regain control of the island. Stores had been seized and, with the enemy in control of the reservoirs, water began to run short.

At mid-afternoon on 25 December – known now as 'Black Christmas' – Maltby advised Young that further resistance would incur nothing but more loss of life. As the

East Brigade was moving in for yet another futile attack, word came of the surrender.

The Commonwealth forces had spent 17 days fighting a force that was considerably more than three times their number. Having little military training and no combat experience, the Canadians had come up against seasoned Japanese soldiers supported by heavy artillery and what appeared to be an unending line of reinforcements. Canada had suffered its first combat casualties of the war – 290 killed and 493 wounded. For more than three and a half more years the killing would continue.

Isogai Rensuke, a general in the Imperial Japanese Army, was installed as the first Japanese governor of Hong Kong. During his tenure, his soldiers terrorized the local population through pillaging, rape and murder. The combat survivors of the Battle of Hong Kong were tortured and starved by their captors. Forced to work in the mines and on the docks, they subsisted on a daily ration of fewer than 800 calories per day.

These and similar atrocities had begun even during the

Battle of Hong Kong. On 24 December, the 16th day of combat, Japanese soldiers had swarmed an improvised hospital, assaulting, raping and murdering nurses; lying in their beds, the wounded Canadian soldiers were bayoneted.

Nearly a third of those 1,975 who left the Port of Vancouver in November 1940 never saw Canada again.

THE RAID *on* DIEPPE

19 AUGUST 1942

—◦—

As THE WINTER of 1942 slowly receded, German fortunes were reaching ever increasing heights. They had infiltrated far into the Soviet Union; with the exception of Egypt, North Africa was theirs. These accomplishments, significant though they were, paled when compared to what had been achieved in Western Europe, where the Allied forces had been pushed back across the English Channel into Great Britain. This stood in contrast with the Great War in which all large territorial gains had ended within the first three months.

Shut out of continental Europe in the last days of 1941, the British began launching a series of raids on German coastal positions. These small excursions, many involving fewer than 1,000 men, had a variety of objectives, from the destruction of stores to the gathering of intelligence. Originated under the Chief of Combined Operations,

Roger Keyes, all had taken place under his successor Louis Mountbatten.

The first planned under the new chief was to have been Operation Rutter, a large-scale raid intended to capture and briefly hold a sizeable port so as to test new equipment and seize materials. Of greater importance, it was believed that, through this particular excursion, experience and information might be gathered which would prove useful in some later, massive amphibious assault. Mountbatten was particularly interested in gauging and studying enemy reaction.

The site chosen for Operation Rutter was Dieppe, a beautiful seaside town and commune that had achieved popularity with English writers and painters of the late 19th century. Built on a long cliff overlooking the English Channel, the city featured a fair-sized harbour that had, centuries earlier, been a key departure point for emigrants to New France.

The plan to use Canada's troops in Operation Rutter was born through growing dissatisfaction among their ranks.

The Canadian forces in Britain, having undergone month after month of training, had been largely inactive, and were eager to experience combat. The attack would be led by the 2nd Canadian Infantry Division and advance inland as far as Arques-la-Bataille, a village some 6 km to the south-east. There were to be two flanking attacks by paratroopers, a naval bombardment and more than 1,000 sorties by Allied air forces.

By 20 May, the 2nd Canadian Infantry Division had been moved to the Isle of Wight, where they continued their training – this time focusing on amphibious operations. Forty-six days later, on 5 July, they boarded ships and prepared for battle. However, on the eve of their departure Luftwaffe bombers swept across the Channel and attacked a flotilla of about 250 Allied ships off Britain's south coast.

It now appeared to the Allied commanders that the raid would likely not come as a surprise. While Field Marshal Bernard Montgomery argued that the venture should be put off indefinitely, within a week Mountbatten went to work on reorganising the raid.

As 'Operation Jubilee', the revived raid was rescheduled for the morning of 19 August. It was to begin just before dawn with four simultaneous flank attacks along a front 16 km in length. Half an hour later would come the main attack on Dieppe itself. This was to be accomplished by the Canadians, who would also hold gaps in the cliffs at Puys, just outside the town, and Pourville, 4 km to the west. Meanwhile, the British Commandos were to destroy flanking coastal batteries at Berneval and Varengeville.

After night fell on the evening of 18 August, more than 250 ships left ports along the British coast. The next morning, still under cover of darkness, the landing craft of the left flank, carrying the British Commandos, encountered S-boats that were protecting a German tanker. The ensuing battle alerted German coastal defences, eliminating any remaining element of surprise. Still at sea, the commandos' craft were torpedoed and became scattered. The majority failed to reach shore.

The few commandos who did land attempted to engage their intended target: a German coastal battery near

Berneval-le-Grand, some 8 km west of Dieppe. Though the destruction of the battery was no longer possible, 18 commandos acting as snipers managed to prevent the German guns from firing on the approaching Allied ships.

It was the commandos on the right flank that had the greatest success of the day. Their destruction of the battery at Varengeville would be the sole objective met in what would soon become the greatest slaughter of Canadian troops in the country's history.

Closer to town, at Puys, the Royal Regiment of Canada had no choice but to land as dawn was breaking, well within the sights of the German mortar and machine guns. On an unexpectedly narrow beach, they struggled and died beneath high cliffs populated by the enemy. While a small number of fortunate soldiers managed to surmount the heavily wired sea wall, others were pinned with no possibility of retreat. More than 200 soldiers were killed; of the remaining 297, only 33 managed to get back across the Channel.

At Pourville, to the west of Dieppe, the Germans were actually taken by surprise. There was little opposition initially, but resistance grew as the Canadians moved eastwards. The advance was soon halted by heavy fighting, and the troops were forced to retreat, leaving all objectives unmet. The withdrawal was only a partial success. As the landing craft arrived, German fire caused death upon the beach. The rearguard became cut off, making evacuation impossible. The Canadians were eventually forced to surrender, having run out of ammunition. Ultimately, failure to clear the areas to the east and west of Dieppe permitted the Germans to fire upon the beaches from both sides, thus nullifying the main frontal attack.

This tragic main assault took place on the steep pebble beach directly in front of the town. Timed to begin half an hour after the attacks to the east and west, the lag really only served the enemy. Having had time to prepare, the Germans had taken up position in buildings overlooking the promenade and atop the cliff.

The assault on the eastern section of the beach by the Essex Scottish Regiment was strafed by machine-gun fire. The sea wall, proving an insurmountable barrier, became a point of death. Incredibly, one platoon managed to enter the town. However, this accomplishment led to further tragedy when the message relayed to headquarters, offshore on HMS *Calpe*, was misinterpreted by Major General J.H. Roberts, commander of the 2nd Canadian Infantry Division. As a result, Les Fusiliers Mont-Royal, a reserve battalion, was ordered on to the beach, only to be pinned down and exposed to German fire. Only 125 of their 584 members returned to Great Britain.

At the west end of the beach, the Royal Hamilton Light Infantry landed and managed to clear pillboxes and a casino being used by the enemy for cover before entering the town itself. Once there, they became bogged down in a vicious street fight.

Much of the prospect for success fell to the King's Own Calgary Regiment, which was to introduce Churchill tanks to the battle. Their landing was to have been covered by a concentrated air and naval bombardment. However, the regiment arrived at the beach ten minutes late. With no support, they were extremely vulnerable. Only 27 of the

58 tanks made it ashore, and of these a dozen were either unable to climb the pebbled incline of the beach, fell victim to the enemy's anti-tank trench or were simply incapable of negotiating the sea wall. The 15 that did manage to bypass the structure were prevented from entering the village by large concrete obstacles that had been used to seal off the narrow streets.

The final landing was made by select members of Britain's Royal Marine 'A' Commando. Like the Canadians before them, the formation suffered heavy losses on the beach. In fact, after hitting land not one of the 369 commandos managed to make it more than a few metres.

Just before 11:00, Roberts ordered a general retreat.

It was here that the tanks proved their greatest value, covering the infantry as they withdrew towards the Channel. Those fighting from within the Churchills either became prisoners of war or were killed.

Those fortunate enough to return did so under cover of the Royal Air Force and the Royal Canadian Air Force, both of whom had provided protection for the British ships moored off the coast of Dieppe. In the air, as on the ground, the losses had been great. The Luftwaffe succeeded in shooting down 13 Royal Canadian Air Force planes and 106 aircraft of the Royal Air Force – the latter would prove to be the highest single-day total for the entire war.

The Canadians who returned to waiting British ships at the end of Operation Jubilee numbered 2,210, approximately 55 per cent of those who reached the beach at Dieppe. A further 1,000 never landed. The total casualties amounted to 3,367, of which 913 had been killed.

The battle over, a debate as to its merit began which continues to this day. For many the Dieppe Raid was a senseless waste of human life, while others argue that the knowledge gained through Operation Jubilee was essential to the success of the D-Day Invasion two years later. The raid is perhaps nowhere more controversial than in Canada. In the country which suffered the greatest losses, Louis Mountbatten is accused of inadequate planning and a failure to communicate. Indeed, the S-boats stumbled upon by the British Commandos had been spotted hours earlier, yet no information was passed down the line.

After the liberation of France, the town of Dieppe came to name several features in honour of the Canadian sacrifice – the Avenue des Canadiens is one of the municipality's major thoroughfares, and the Dieppe-Canada Monument is located in the Square du Canada, just south of where the Canadians first landed. A feature of the tribute is a cast plaque which reads:

Le dix-neuf août mil neuf cent quarante-deux sur la plage de Dieppe nos cousins canadiens tracèrent de leur sang la voie de notre libération finale présageant ainsi leur retour victorieux du premier septembre mil neuf cent quarante-quatre.

THE BATTLE *of* ORTONA
20–28 DECEMBER 1943

———

'**B**LOODY DECEMBER' is the name given to the fighting on the Adriatic front during the closing weeks of 1943. For Canada, it is a description that seems particularly appropriate. During that month, the Canadian forces in Italy suffered 1,375 dead. Of these, 213 were killed in a particularly brutal urban battle fought over a seven-day period – one of which included Christmas Day.

The setting for all this death was Ortona, a small picturesque town of 10,000 inhabitants, first settled during the Bronze Age. Its main feature, a deep water port, lent the town great strategic importance.

Events leading directly to the Battle of Ortona began on 23 November with a British Eighth Army offensive on a specific fortification the German military had built in Italy. The Winter Line was, in fact, not one but a series of seven lines of fortification that ran from the Adriatic to the

Tyrrhenian seas. The Eighth Army assault had been on the central Gustav Line, considered the main line. Constructed along the Rapido and Garigliano rivers, it featured barbed wire, minefields, machine-gun nests and concrete bunkers.

Under then-commander Bernard Montgomery, the Eighth Army managed to overcome many of these obstacles, and by the end of the month had penetrated the main Gustav Line defences. As Allied forces advanced northwards towards the Moro river, the 1st Canadian Infantry Division took over the right flank, that closest to the Adriatic Sea.

Throughout their push to Ortona, the Canadians were forced to contend with a cold, heavy rain, weather which made the land surrounding the town difficult to negotiate.

Montgomery had believed that the Germans at Ortona would give up the town and retreat to the Arielli river, 5 km to the north, which afforded excellent positions for defence. Moreover, less than a year earlier, the Germans had been taught the harshest of lessons at the Battle of Stalingrad. After that defeat, it was assumed by Montgomery and others that the enemy would avoid urban warfare whenever possible. Finally, there was a distinct possibility that the German supply line to Ortona might soon be severed. Montgomery recognized this truth and, again, assumed that the Germans did as well.

Ortona was held, in the main, by the German 1st Parachute Division, a fanatical, elite formation with a well-earned reputation as one of the country's most formidable forces. They had prepared for the Canadian assault on the town by destroying the port. The Germans erected barricades in the side streets leading to the central Piazza Municipale. Booby traps, time bombs, machine-gun nests and anti-tank emplacements were installed throughout the town. Many of the buildings had been collapsed so as to create rubble which would prevent tanks from advancing through Ortona's maze of streets. Other thoroughfares were blocked off for the purposes of channelling the advancing enemy into kill zones. Adding to this labyrinth and to the German advantage was the presence of countless underground passages connected to the cellars of homes and other buildings in the older section of the town.

The Canadian assault began on 20 December with a heavy artillery barrage which served to cover the Loyal Edmonton Regiment and elements of the Seaforth Highlanders of Canada as they moved into the town. Their attempt to dislodge the occupying Germans was met with resistance that was both efficient and vicious. From the buildings that had been left standing, the Canadians came under fire from the snipers whom they could not see. Making use of their 6-pounder (2.5 kg) guns, the Canadians fired on walls and rooftops – wherever they thought the enemy might be concealed. When walls proved too thick to pierce, they aimed at windows in an attempt to shoot shells directly into the structure.

Taking refuge in buildings, the Canadians developed a new tactic they called 'mouse-holing'. This involved creating passages within buildings, most often with the aid of a pickaxe or explosive device, which allowed for the movement through blocks of the town without risk of exposure or observation.

Despite their innovation, the Canadians made slow progress. Each edifice entered held the risk of trip wires and charges. Twenty-three members of the Loyal Edmonton Regiment were killed in an explosion that occurred just moments after they had entered a new building.

In the midst of the carnage, the Seaforth Highlanders and some of the more fortunate members of the Loyal Edmontons celebrated Christmas with a banquet laid out in the Church of Santa Maria di Constandinopoli.

Two days later, the Princess Patricia Canadian Light Infantry and the Régiment de Trois-Rivières joined in the battle.

The exhausted Germans benefited from no such relief. With their supply line cut and no hope of reinforcements, they were a depleted force. On 27 December, after a week of fighting, they withdrew under the cover of night, leaving their dead behind.

Canadian losses in this, their most urban engagement of the war, amounted to more than 100 dead, more than ten for each day of the battle. Roughly one quarter of all Canadian casualties in the Italian Campaign occurred in the town of Ortona.

The confusion wrought by urban warfare, combined with a hastened retreat and the fanatical pride of the German 1st Parachute Regiment has obscured the number of German casualties. It is estimated that between 100 and 200 Germans died in the Battle of Ortona. In all likelihood, at least 48 of these deaths occurred on 26 December when a structure housing the paratroopers was brought down by Canadian engineers.

The Battle of Ortona is generally considered to have been the deadliest close-quarter engagement of the war. Due to the great loss of life and the use of mouse-holing, the clash is sometimes referred to as 'Little Stalingrad', a name coined by journalist Matthew Halton.

THE D-DAY LANDINGS
6 JUNE 1944

————•————

THERE WERE D-DAYS before the 1944 Allied invasion of Normandy. Uncertain in both origin and meaning, the term has been traced back to the First World War when it was used in a field order by the American Expeditionary Forces. However, the achievement, magnitude and consequence of 6 June 1944 has ensured that it remains *the* D-Day.

The largest seaborne invasion, it involved more than 156,000 troops from the United Kingdom, the United States, Canada and the Forces Françaises Libres. Nearly 7,000 vessels of all types would be involved, more than 4,000 of which were landing craft. Approximately 12,000 aircraft would be used in supporting the landings, a task which included attack sorties, the dropping of bombs and the transportation of parachute troops.

The objective of the invasion, the creation of a lodgement

in Western Europe, was long held and thought essential to the defeat of Germany. Since 1942, plans had been drawn and redrawn, eventually emerging as 'Operation Neptune', the assault phase, and 'Operation Overlord', the invasion itself.

The ultimate site chosen for the landing was the Cotentin Caen area of the Normandy coast, approximately 350 km to the south-west of the Pas de Calais, where the Germans stood in anticipation, fooled by the Allies' deception operations. While this would require a lengthier and more hazardous passage for the invading fleet, those landing would find the beaches more accommodating and the enemy presence and defences lighter.

The invasion plans (see plate section) called for a wide landing in which five infantry divisions, each dedicated to a specific beach, would wade ashore along an 80-km stretch of the Normandy coast. Units of the 1st Canadian Army would join with the British Second Army in forming the left side of the assault, while the 1st United States Army would take the right. They would be preceded by three airborne divisions, including members of the 1st Canadian Parachute

Battalion, all intended to impede German movements, thereby allowing the establishment of a beachhead.

Two brigades of the 3rd Canadian Infantry Divisions were to land in the first wave at Juno Beach, one of the two most heavily fortified beaches targeted in the assault.

The Canadian units were charged with establishing a beachhead, capturing the three small towns which lay directly behind it, before advancing inland to take position on the high ground west of the city of Caen.

More than 15,000 Canadians would take part as actual members of the landing force, while the remaining elements of the First Canadian Army would be expected to move in on Normandy in the weeks that followed.

Although the location of the landing would come as a surprise, the Germans, weakened after five years of war and battered by the Soviet Union, were well aware that an invasion was imminent. In 1942, as the planning of an invasion was in its earliest stages, they had begun work on the *Atlantikwall*, an extensive system of coastal fortifications, in anticipation of just such an attack. Stretching from the Atlantic border between Spain and France to the northernmost territory of Norway, the wall consisted of artillery, mines, barbed wire, bunkers, mortar pits, machine-gun nests and beach obstacles. Beginning early in 1944 under the guidance of Field Marshal Erwin Rommel, the wall had been strengthened further through the construction of a line of reinforced-concrete pillboxes.

The D-Day Invasion was to have taken place on 5 June but storms forced a postponement, despite the fact that several ships were already at sea. The forecast looked grim; meteorologists predicted only marginally favourable weather for the following day. The decision to proceed fell to Supreme Commander of the Allied Forces Dwight D. Eisenhower, who recognized that, given the tides, another month would pass before conditions were again right for invasion. This judgement, questioned privately by some in command, was shown to increase the element of surprise. The Germans were certain that no invasion could take place for at least several days. Rommel himself saw the inclement weather as an opportunity to take a few days' leave.

The field marshal was with his family when, in the early hours of 6 June, the first Allied forces reached Normandy. Paratroopers, including 450 Canadians, landed behind the *Atlantikwall*. Though greatly outnumbered, they managed to create havoc and confusion within the German ranks; a headquarters was seized, a key bridge was destroyed and transportation links were severed.

All this was taking place as Canadian landing craft were approaching the Normandy coast. It was just after eight o'clock that the Regina Rifles became the first to land. Their advance on the beach was covered by the tanks of the 1st Hussars, a piece of good fortune, as a great many German defensive positions had survived preliminary bombardments. Together, they managed to fight their way off the beach and into the town of Courseulles-sur-Mer. By late afternoon they were able to advance inland.

Supported by accurate naval gunfire, the Victoria's Canadian Scottish landed successfully at Mike sector and members of the Royal Winnipeg Rifles – the Little Black Devils – came under enemy gunfire while still far offshore.

Many were killed as they left the landing craft. Some of those who made it to land managed to advance past the beach defences, where they occupied the nearby coastal villages.

If anything, the Nan sector proved less inviting as bombardment from the Channel had failed to dent German defences. One particular concrete bunker destroyed several tanks of the Fort Garry Horse and brought heavy casualties to the North Shore Regiment before being silenced.

It was in this sector that the Queen's Own Rifles would receive the worst battering of any Canadian unit. Although their landing was to have been preceded by DD tanks, this was not possible due to high waves. The Queen's Own arrived at the beach more than half an hour behind schedule. Although they arrived pretty much intact, the killing began almost immediately. With no cover whatsoever, the Canadians were forced to scramble from the shoreline to the seawall, a distance of more than 180 m. Two-thirds of their number were cut down by a German 88-mm gun.

A second company of the Queen's Own had the

misfortune of hitting the beach directly opposite a German strongpoint. Half of those who landed were killed, before the Germans themselves became casualties.

The experience of the Queen's Own stands in contrast with that of the Canadian Scottish, who arrived in the second wave. While the Canadian Scottish suffered fewer casualties than any other battalion, their fellow reserve unit, Le Régiment de la Chaudière's, were not nearly so lucky. As they approached the coast, the Chaudière's landing craft struck a concealed mine. As a result, the Quebec regiment had no choice but to abandon their equipment and attempt a swim to shore.

Of the Canadian units involved in the invasion, only one managed to reach their D-Day objective. Nevertheless, they had left the first line of enemy defences in ruins. As dusk set, the Canadians had advanced farther inland than any other of the invading forces. Three hundred and forty Canadians died, with another 574 wounded. Forty-seven Canadians were taken prisoner.

With the great drama that took place on the beaches of Normandy, the contributions of those in the air and at sea are sometimes overlooked.

The Royal Canadian Air Force, who had for several months been bombing key German targets in the Normandy area, were among the first to see action. While Canadian fighter pilots took on the Luftwaffe, the No. 6 Bomber Group dropped several thousand tonnes of explosives on coastal defences.

In the English Channel, minesweepers of the Royal Canadian Navy worked to clear the path to Normandy. Canadian destroyers fired their guns to add to the destruction of coastal defences wrought by the air force.

With their British and American allies, the Canadians were soon able to establish a continuous front. The *Atlantikwall* had been breached.

CHAPTER X

—•◆•—

The Post-War Era

THE
POST-WAR
ERA
1945–PRESENT DAY

An introduction

WITH THE END of the Second World War, Canada rapidly demobilized. And yet not five years after the end of the Second World War, Canada was joining in the fight against the North in the Korean War. More than 500 Canadian lives were lost in the conflict which, when over, appeared to fade from public memory.

The country had already entered into a golden age of diplomacy, led by the future prime minister Lester B. Pearson, among others. Peacekeeping became the focus of the military. Beginning with the first in 1957, until 1989 Canada participated in every United Nations peacekeeping mission. Iin the 1990s, however, participation decreased greatly. Once among the ten greatest contributors of military personnel to United Nations peacekeeping missions, by 2006 Canada could no longer be counted in the top fifty.

It wasn't until the 1991 Gulf War that Canadians again participated in combat operations. One of a coalition of 34 nations to fight Iraq, Canada contributed a field hospital, a CF-18 squadron, a supply ship, and the destroyers HMCS *Athabaskan*, *Huron* and *Terra Nova*. The Gulf War holds the distinction of being the only war in which Canada suffered no casualties.

Another decade passed before the war in Afghanistan and Canada would again send troops into combat.

THE BATTLE *of* KAP'YONG

22–25 APRIL 1951

MORE THAN ANY other conflict in Canada's story, the Korean War is the 'forgotten war'. Indeed, it is frequently referred to as such by historians in many of the participating nations. Beginning less than five years after the end of the Second World War, the death and destruction experienced between 1950 and 1953 on the Korean Peninsula was easily overshadowed by that great conflict. And yet, the Second World War spawned the Korean War; the division of the once unified country by occupying forces of the Soviet Union and the United States proved a failure. The supposed objective of later unification fell apart in the growing tensions between the former allies.

This war in the Land of the Morning Calm began before dawn on 25 June 1950, when 135,000 soldiers of the North Korean People's Army crossed the 38th parallel into South Korea and proceeded along the Ouijongbu corridor en route to Seoul. It took less than three days for the North Koreans to capture the South Korean capital.

Under the banner of the United Nations, 16 countries sent troops to aid South Korea's army. The first to land were the Americans. By this point, the North Koreans had captured Seoul and were advancing on the southern port city of Pusan. Fierce fighting stemmed the northern tide, and by the end of September United Nations troops had taken Seoul. In January, the city was again lost, this time to a North Korean force strengthened by the 2,300,000-strong Chinese People's Volunteer Army.

The previous month, the first contingent of Canadians, the 2nd Battalion, Princess Patricia's Canadian Light Infantry arrived in Korea.

On 22 April, the People's Volunteer Army launched its 'Fifth Phase Offensive', a major operation, which involved three field armies numbering more than 700,000 troops. Their objective was the recapture of Seoul, which they had lost the previous month.

The People's 118th Division of the People's Volunteer

Army led the operation and attacked broadly along the entire front, eventually breaking the line by forcing the withdrawal of American and South Korean forces.

The following day, the Patricias moved from a rest area some 25 km to the south to establish defensive positions on Hill 677, a feature within corps reserve, 20 km behind the lines.

In the first minutes of 24 June, a force of 6,000 Chinese attacked Australian positions throughout the Kap'yong valley. Lasting some sixteen hours, this first phase of the Battle of Kap'yong involved wave after wave of Chinese assault troops. Eventually, running low on ammunition, the Australians were forced to withdraw.

Left alone to halt the Chinese advance, one Patricias' company took up position in an abandoned village opposite the ground once held by the Australians. From the limited protection offered by small, thatched-roof huts, they engaged the approaching Chinese, before having to retreat.

As they attempted to ford the Kap'yong, the People's Volunteer Army were fired upon from Canadian positions, leaving more than 70 Chinese dead.

At approximately one o'clock on the morning of 25 April, a Canadian platoon was attacked by Chinese troops, resulting in hand-to-hand combat. Clearly outnumbered and in danger of being overrun, Captain Walter Mills, the company commander, requested that local New Zealand artillery fire on his position. As the Canadians laid low in their trenches, shells swept along the ground at the Chinese. When they returned, artillery fire was again requested. A total of 2,300 rounds rained down on the company's position.

Two hours before dawn, the Chinese assault on Hill 677 was abandoned. Now isolated, the Canadians were left with severely depleted ammunition and rations. It was only through air-dropped supplies that the Patricias were able to be properly readied for the resumption of battle. However, the expected assaults never materialized; the Chinese had suffered heavy casualties and had outdistanced their supply line. The Battle of Kap'yong had come to an end with the failure of the Chinese to exploit their breach of the United Nations line.

The Canadian victory over the People's Volunteer Army meant that Seoul would never again be threatened.

Canadian losses at the Battle of Kap'yong were light, particularly when compared to those of the Chinese. While ten members of the Patricias were killed and 23 injured, it is generally accepted that deaths among the People's Volunteer Army amounted to more than 1,000.

While officially the war continues to this day, combat ended on 27 July 1953 with the signing of the Korean Armistice Agreement.

In more than three years of fierce fighting, 6,000,000 Koreans were killed. Close to 500,000 Chinese soldiers of the People's Liberation Army died in combat. The Canadians killed numbered 516, with more than 1,000 wounded.

Canadian troops remained in South Korea for several years after the armistice; the last to leave, the Canadian Medical Detachment, sailed in June 1957 from Inchon.

After more than half a century, the ceasefire continues to hold.

THE SECOND BATTLE *of* PANJWAYE

2–17 SEPTEMBER 2006

———•———

O N 7 OCTOBER 2001, less than four weeks after the 11 September terrorist attacks on the United States, Prime Minister Jean Chrétien announced that Canada would be contributing forces for two years in an international effort to conduct a campaign against terrorism. In fact, Canadian forces continued combat for ten years until finally withdrawing in 2011, leaving a unit of military trainers to work with the Afghan security forces.

Two months after Canada joined the war, in early December 2001, 40 members of the Canadian Forces' elite special-operations unit, Joint Task Force Two, were sent as part of the Special Operations coalition in Afghanistan. They were joined in mid-January 2002 by the first of some 700 members of the regular forces.

In March, elements of Joint Task Force Two and the Princess Patricia's Canadian Light Infantry formed part of a multinational force in Operation Anaconda. This effort to destroy Taliban and al-Qaeda forces in Afghanistan's eastern Paktia Province marked the first large-scale battle of the war to include Canadian forces.

The early months of the Canadian mission were marred when, on 18 April 2002, an American F-16 dropped a laser-guided bomb on a group of Canadian soldiers who were conducting night-time training on a designated live-fire range outside Kabul. This friendly-fire incident caused the first Canadian deaths in a military campaign since that of William Patrick Regan, a private in the Korean War, 49 years earlier. Eight other Canadians were wounded.

Expanded and extended, the role of the Canadian mission in Afghanistan underwent a major change in February 2006 when it assumed command from the American forces in Kandahar Province in southern Afghanistan. The Canadians moved into the province at a time when violence was on the rise. This was particularly true in the Panjwaye, a rural district in the west.

In May 2006, at about the time the mission was again extended, the growing violence was countered by Operation Mountain Thrust, the largest offensive since the fall of the Taliban more than five years earlier. Commanded by the United States and led jointly by Americans and Canadians, it involved approximately 3,500 Afghan soldiers, with a further 7,800 troops from the United States, Canada and the United Kingdom.

Close to the beginning of the operation, on 17 May, a number of fire fights took place between the Canadians and Taliban insurgents. One of these took the life of Captain Nichola Goddard, the first female Canadian soldier in any conflict to be killed in combat.

On 12 July, intense fighting broke out in a series of mud-wall complexes held by Taliban forces. Though the First Battle of Panjwaye ended in a victory for Canadian and Afghan forces, the Taliban did not leave the Panjwaye, nor did their influence dissipate. In the weeks that followed,

Taliban forces returned in even greater number.

Operation Medusa, a Canadian-led offensive of approximately 2,000 troops from Canada, the United Kingdom, the United States, the Netherlands, Denmark and the Afghan National Army, began on the morning of 2 September. Intended to establish government control in Kandahar Province, the action was directed towards the town of Panjwaye.

On the second day, NATO reported that 200 suspected Taliban insurgents had been killed. Casualties among the Canadians had also been high. Three were killed in an assault on a Taliban position, while a fourth was killed in a bomb attack. On the morning of 4 September, a Canadian soldier was killed and more than 30 others were wounded when an American A-10 Thunderbolt II accidentally strafed the very same troops who had called in the air support.

From the very beginning the Canadians encountered heavy fighting, but this ended abruptly on 11 September, the fifth anniversary of the terrorist attacks on New York and Washington. The Taliban had begun a retreat from the battlefield, leaving behind a large number of booby traps. As the Canadians advanced into areas the Taliban had once controlled, they encountered only sporadic resistance; an expected last stand never materialized.

The Canadians suffered 12 deaths; the Netherlands and the United States each lost one soldier. It was the British who experienced the greatest loss of life. On the first day of the offensive, one of their Nimrod MR2 reconnaissance aircraft crashed, killing all 14 on board. The greatest single-incident loss of life for the British in Afghanistan, it is not believed to have been a result of hostile action.

On 17 September, NATO announced that Operation Medusa had been ended.

The following day, in the village of Char Kota, Pashmul, a male cyclist approached Canadian soldiers who were handing out presents. He detonated a vest rigged with explosives, killing four soldiers, wounding several more, and injuring two dozen Afghan children.

BIBLIOGRAPHY

Allen, Robert S., *The Loyal Americans: The Military Rôle of the Loyalist Provincial Corps and Their Settlement in British North America, 1775–1784*, Ottawa: National Museum of Man/ National Museums of Canada, 1983.

Beal, Bob, 'Lief Newry Fitzroy Crozier' in *The Dictionary of Canadian Biography: Volume XIII, 1901–1910*, Toronto: University of Toronto Press, 1994.

Beasley, David R., *The Canadian Don Quixote: The Life and Works of Major John Richardson, Canada's First Novelist*, Erin, Ont.: Porcupine's Quill, 1977.

Beauclerk, Charles, *Lithographic Views of Military Operations in Canada During the Late Insurrection*, London: A. Flint, 1840.

Berton, Pierre, *Flames Across the Border*, Toronto: McClelland & Stewart, 1981.

—, *The Invasion of Canada*, Toronto: McClelland & Stewart, 1980.

Blakeley, Phyllis R. and John N. Grant, *Eleven Exiles: Accounts of Loyalists of the American Revolution*, Toronto: Dundurn, 1982.

Bradford, Robert D., *Historic Forts of Ontario*, Belleville, Ont.: Mika, 1988.

Bradley, A. G., *The Fight with France for North America*, London: Constable, 1902.

Busby, Brian, *Character Parts: Who's Really Who in Can Lit*, Toronto: Knopf Canada, 2003.

— (ed.), *In Flanders Fields and Other Poems of the First World War*, London: Arcturus, 2005.

Champlain, Samuel de, *Voyages of Samuel de Champlain: 1604–1618*, Boston: The Prince Society, 1887.

Chartrand, René, *French Fortresses in North America 1535–1763: Québec, Montréal, Louisbourg and New Orleans*, Oxford: Osprey, 2005.

Colombo, John Robert, *Colombo's All Time Great Canadian Quotations*. Toronto: Stoddart, 1994.

Cruikshank, E. A. (ed.), *The Documentary History of the Campaign upon the Niagara Frontier, 1812–1814*, 9 vols. Welland, Ont.: Lundy's Lane Historical Society, 1896–1908.

Dallison, Robert E., *Turning Back the Fenians: New Brunswick's Last Colonial Campaign*, Fredericton: Goose Lane, 2006.

Dempsey, Hugh A., 'Potikwahanapiwoyin (Poundmaker)' in *The Dictionary of Canadian Biography: Volume XI, 1881–1890*, Toronto: University of Toronto Press, 1982.

Dunnigan, James F. and Albert A. Nofi, *Dirty Little Secrets of World War II*, New York: Morrow, 1994.

Elting, John R., *Amateurs to Arms! A Military History of the War of 1812*, Chapell Hill, N.C.: Algonquin, 1991.

English, John, *Borden: His Life and World*, Toronto: McGraw-Hill Ryerson, 1977.

—, 'The Fenian Folly.' *The New York Times*, 5 June 1866.

FitzGibbon, Mary Agnes, *A Veteran of 1812: The Life of James FitzGibbon*, Toronto: Prospero, 2000.

Flint, David, *John Strachan: Pastor and Politician*, Toronto: Oxford University Press, 1971.

—, *William Lyon Mackenzie: Rebel Against Authority*, Toronto: Oxford University Press, 1971.

Fortier, John, 'Augustin de Boschenry de Drocour' in *The Dictionary of Canadian Biography: Volume III, 1741–1770*,

Toronto: University of Toronto Press, 1974.

Fussell, Paul, *The Great War and Modern Memory*, New York: Oxford University Press, 1975.

Gall, Carlotta, 'Attacks in Afghanistan Grow More Frequent and Lethal', *The New York Times*, 27 Sep 2006.

—, 'New Assault Takes Big Toll on Taliban, NATO Says', *The New York Times*, 4 Sep 2006.

—, 'Taliban Surges as US Shifts Some Tasks to NATO', *The New York Times*, 11 June 2006.

Graham, Dominick, 'Charles Lawrence' in *The Dictionary of Canadian Biography: Volume III, 1741–1770*, Toronto: University of Toronto Press, 1974.

Graves, Donald E., *Guns Across the River: The Battle of the Windmill*, Prescott, Ontario: Friends of Windmill Point/ Robin Brass Studio, 2001.

—, *Redcoats and Grey Jackets: The Battle of Chippawa, 5 July 1814*, Toronto: Dundurn, 1994.

—, *Where Right and Glory Lead! The Battle of Lundy's Lane, 1814*, Toronto: Robin Brass Studio, 1997.

— (ed), *Fighting for Canada: Seven Battles, 1758–1945*, Toronto:

Robin Brass Studio, 2000.

— (ed), *More Fighting for Canada: Five Battles, 1760–1944*, Toronto: Robin Brass Studio, 2000.

Guitard, Michelle, 'Charles-Michel d'Irumberry de Salaberry' in *The Dictionary of Canadian Biography: Volume VI, 1821–1835*, Toronto: University of Toronto Press, 1987.

Gwyn, Julian, 'Edward Whitmore' in *The Dictionary of Canadian Biography: Volume III, 1741–1770*, Toronto: University of Toronto Press, 1974.

Hibbert, Christopher, *Wolfe at Quebec*. London: Longmans, Green, 1959.

Hitsman, J. Mackay, *The Incredible War of 1812: A Military History*, Toronto: Robin Brass Studio, 1999.

Laurier, Wilfrid, *Wilfrid Laurier on the Platform*, Compiled by Ulrich Barthe, Quebec: Turcotte & Menard, 1890.

Leblanc, Daniel, and Shawn McCarthy, 'US Jet Bombs Canadians', *The Globe & Mail*, 18 Apr 2002.

Lighthall, W. D., *An Account of the Battle of Châteauguay; Being a Lecture Delivered at Ormstown, March 8th, 1889*, Montreal:

Drysdale, 1889.

Lloyd, Christopher, *The Capture of Quebec*, London: Batsford, 1959.

Lossing, Benson J., *The Pictorial Field-Book of the War of 1812*, New York: Harper & Brothers, 1868.

Macdonald, John A, *Troublous Times in Canada: A History of the Fenian Raids of 1866 and 1970*, Toronto: W.S. Johnston, 1910.

Mackenzie, William Lyon, *The Selected Writings, 1824–1837*, Toronto: Oxford University Press, 1960.

Mason, Christopher, 'Canadian Seeks to Defend Losses in Afghanistan', *The New York Times*, 28 Sep 2006.

McCrae, John, *In Flanders Fields*, Toronto: Briggs, 1919.

Meighen, Arthur, *Oversea Addresses, June – July 1921*, Toronto: Musson, 1921.

Morton, Desmond, *A Military History of Canada (Fifth Edition)*, Toronto: McClelland & Stewart, 2007.

—, and J.L., Granatstein, *Marching to Armageddon: Canadians and the Great War 1914-1919*, Toronto: Lester & Orpen Denys, 1989

— (ed), *The Queen vs. Louis Riel*, Toronto: University of Toronto Press, 1974.

Nasmith, George G., *In the Fringe of the Great Fight*, Toronto: McClelland, Goodchild & Stewart, 1917.

Neidardt, W. S., *Fenianism in North America*, University Park, PA: Pennsylvania State University Press, 1975.

Nelson, Wolfred, *Écrits d'une patriote, 1812–1842*, Montreal: Comeau & Nadeau, 1998.

Nowlan, Alden, Campobello: *The Outer Island*, Toronto: Clarke, Irwin, 1975.

Pariseau, Jean, 'Jean-Baptiste-Nicolas-Roch de Ramezay' in *The Dictionary of Canadian Biography: Volume IV, 1771–1800*, Toronto: University of Toronto Press, 1979.

Parkman, Francis, *Montcalm and Wolfe*, New York: Collier, 1962.

Perreaux, Les, 'Four Canadians Killed, Six Wounded in Afghan Battle', *The Globe & Mail*, 3 Sep 2006.

—, 'Friendly Fire Claims Another Canadian', *The Globe & Mail*, 4 Sep 2006.

Pothier, Bernard, 'Louis Du Pont Duchambon de Vergor' in

The Dictionary of Canadian Biography: Volume IV, 1771–1800, Toronto: University of Toronto Press, 1979.

Read, Daphne, *The Great War and Canadian Society: An Oral History*, Toronto: New Hogtown, 1978.

Richardson, John, *Richardson's War of 1812*, Toronto: Historical Publishing Co., 1902.

Roland, Charles G., 'Massacre and Rape in Hong Kong: Two Case Studies Involving Medical Personnel and Patients', *Journal of Contemporary History, 32:1*. (Jan., 1997): 43–61.

Scott, Frederick George, *The Great War As I Saw It*, Toronto: Goodchild, 1922.

Senior, Hereward, *The Fenians and Canada*, Toronto: Macmillan of Canada, 1978.

—, *The Last Invasion of Canada: The Fenian Raids, 1866–1870*, Toronto: Dundurn, 1991.

Slattery, T.P., *The Assassination of D'Arcy McGee*, Toronto: Doubleday Canada, 1968.

Smith, Graeme, 'Canadians Bloodied, But Unbowed', *The Globe & Mail*, 4 Sep 2006.

—, 'US Error Kills Canadian, Stalls Attack on Taliban', *The Globe & Mail*, 5 Sep 2006.

Stacey, C.P., 'Jefferey Amherst, 1st Baron Amherst' in *The Dictionary of Canadian Biography: Volume IV, 1771–1800*, Toronto: University of Toronto Press, 1979.

Stanley, George F.G., *The War of 1812: Land Operations*, Toronto: Macmillan of Canada, 1983.

Steele, Samuel, *Forty Years in Canada: Reminiscences of the Great Northwest, with Some Account of His Service in South Africa*, Toronto: Prospero, 2000.

Stokesbury, James L., *A Short History of the American Revolution*, New York: Morrow, 1991.

Sugden, John, *Tecumseh: A Life*, New York: Holt, 1997.

Suthern, Victor, *The War of 1812*, Toronto: McClelland & Stewart, 1999.

Swift, Michael, *Historical Maps of Canada*, Toronto: Prospero, 2001.

Villa, Brian Lorring, *Unauthorized Action: Mountbatten and the Dieppe Raid*, Toronto: Oxford University Press, 1991.

Zuehlke, Mark, *The Canadian Military Atlas: The Nation's*

Battlefields from the French and Indian Wars to Kosovo, Toronto: Stoddart, 2001.

—. *For Honour's Sake: The War of 1812 and the Brokering of an Uneasy Peace*. Toronto: Knopf Canada, 2007.

PICTURE CREDITS

Plate section:

All images courtesy of Libraries and Archive Canada